ENGRAVED BY T.B.WELCH. —— THE ORIGINAL BY JOHN NEAGLE.

Saml: Miller

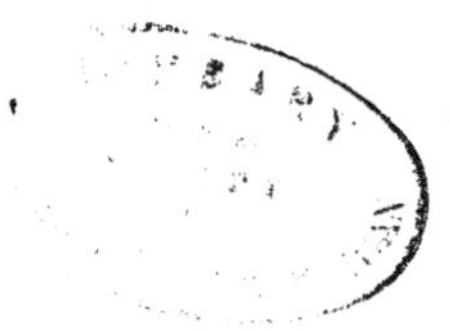

LETTERS

FROM A FATHER

TO

HIS SONS IN COLLEGE.

BY SAMUEL MILLER, D. D.

PROFESSOR IN THE THEOLOGICAL SEMINARY, PRINCETON, NEW JERSEY.

Qui studet optatam cursu contingere metam,
Multa tulit fecitque puer, sudavit et alsit.
HOR. *de Art. Poet.*

Pudore et liberalitate liberos
Retinere, satius esse credo, quám metu.
TERENCE.

PHILADELPHIA:
PRESBYTERIAN BOARD OF PUBLICATION,
No. 265 CHESTNUT STREET.

Stereotyped by SLOTE & MOONEY, Philadelphia.

WM. S. MARTIEN, Printer.

DEDICATION.

To every Parent who has a son in college; and to every Son who is placed in that interesting and responsible situation, this volume is affectionately inscribed. The former may, perhaps, learn from it to estimate more justly his power, though afar off, to contribute toward averting the dangers, and promoting the improvement, of one unspeakably dear to him: and the latter, if he is not blind to his own honour and happiness, and reckless to all the claims of his friends, his Alma Mater, his Country and his God, will certainly find in it counsels not unworthy of his most serious regard.

ADVERTISEMENT.

THE writer of this volume has had five sons trained and graduated in the College of New Jersey. The following Letters, not, indeed, precisely in their present form, but in substance, were actually addressed to them. There is, probably, not one idea contained in this manual which was not, during their course in that Institution, distinctly communicated to them, either orally or in writing. The influence of these counsels on their minds, it is believed, was not wholly useless. May they prove still more useful when presented in this revised and more public form!

PRINCETON, March 30, 1843.

CONTENTS.

LETTERS, &c.

LETTER I.

INTRODUCTORY.

My Dear Sons—You have escaped from the place and the name of *school-boys*, and have become members of a *college;* a college not only venerable for its age and standing, but also famous as the *Alma Mater* of a large number of the most eminent men that have ever adorned our country. This step will, no doubt, form an important era in your lives; perhaps more important than either you or I now anticipate. In placing you in this new and responsible situation, my feelings have been peculiar and solemn. I have looked back upon my own college course, in another institution,* with mingled emotions. The retrospect of its advantages, its pleasing associations, both with teachers and fellow students, and the protection and guidance with which I was favoured by a merciful Providence, at that season of youthful inexperience and peril, never fail to inspire gratitude. But the recollection of my mistakes, my failures, my incorrect estimate of the value of some of my prescribed studies and pursuits, my loss of precious opportunities, and my false steps, at that critical period of my life, is always connected with self-reproach. A thousand times have I said, "O, if I had known as much as I now know of the value of certain studies, and the

* Dr. Miller was a graduate of the University of Pennsylvania, located in Philadelphia.—Editor.

wisdom of certain courses of conduct earnestly recommended to me by parents and friends—how unspeakably more might I have profited by the privileges which I was then permitted to enjoy!"

Can you wonder, then, my dear sons, that I am deeply anxious for your welfare and improvement in the new situation in which I have thought it my duty to place you? And can you doubt that I am ardently desirous of imparting to you a portion of my early experience? Some of that experience was dearly bought. If you are willing and docile you may receive the advantages of it upon easier terms. The importance of parental instruction and discipline is founded on the fact, that every successive individual of our species comes into the world ignorant, feeble and helpless; and that the same process for instilling knowledge into the mind, and for restraining the passions, and correcting the evil propensities of our nature, must be undergone, *de novo*, in every instance. If you could start with the knowledge and the experience with which the aged leave off, you would stand less in need of instruction and exhortation from those who have gone before you; but as this is impossible, you must be content to acquire knowledge, and to gain the mastery over your corrupt propensities, in the way appointed by a gracious God for our fallen race.

Listen, then, to a father who loves you most sincerely; who will never willingly give you a delusive counsel; who prays that you may be inspired with heavenly wisdom; and who can have no greater pleasure than to see you pursuing a course adapted to render you in the highest degree useful, beloved and happy in this world, and for ever blessed in that more important world which is to come.

But beside my natural affection for you, and my tender interest in your welfare, there are other considerations which present a claim to your attention to the counsels contained in these letters. I am the son, as you know, of a minister of the gospel, who passed through a long life devoted to the acquirement and the communication of the best of all knowledge, and who left me many precious counsels, the result of his experience, from which I should have been inexcusable had I not derived some profit. I have myself now lived more than three score and ten years, and, of course, have had much opportunity of observing the conduct and the end of many young men who enjoyed the advantages now conferred on you. I have myself passed through a college course, and, consequently, know something of the character, the habits, and the temptations of college life. I have been a trustee of the college with which you are connected between thirty and forty years, and, in discharging the duties of this office, have become intimately acquainted with the docility, the diligence, and the success of one class of students; and with the aberrations, the discipline, the degrading habits, and the ultimate destruction of another class. It would be strange, indeed, if one who had enjoyed advantages, and passed through scenes of this kind, should not be in some degree qualified to administer warning and caution to those who are beginning a course so momentous to each individual as that on which you have entered. And it would be supposing peculiar perverseness and infatuation on your part, to doubt whether you ought to regard with some respect the counsels of such a friend.

It has occurred to me, too, that by embodying and presenting a few paternal counsels, I may, by the divine blessing, not only profit *you;* but by offering them to the public, from the press, become instrumental in conferring benefits on the children of some of my beloved friends similarly situated with yourselves; and possibly the children of others, whose faces I never saw, and never shall see in the flesh, may not be wholly unprofited by the counsels of an old man, who was once in their situation, and whose duty and happiness it is to promote the welfare of ingenuous youth, wherever and whenever they may be placed within his reach.

I acknowledge, also, I am not without some hope that another benefit may result from the preparation of this manual. I am persuaded that some, at least, of the young men whose disorders in college degrade themselves, distress their parents, and give trouble to their teachers, are betrayed into their ill conduct more by thoughtlessness, by inexperience, and by ignorance of the world, than by any fixed purpose of insubordination or rebellion. They become delinquents more from inadvertence and juvenile folly, than from settled design; and, of course, what they chiefly need is to have their attention called to a variety of subjects, connected with college discipline, and college duty, in regard to which their views and habits are at present erroneous, chiefly because they have never seriously considered them; and have never been taught better. The benefit of such young men is not only earnestly to be desired, but their case is far from being hopeless. There is every prospect that discreet and well directed efforts may make an impression conducive to their permanent good. If therefore, while I put *you* on your guard against the company and the influence of such young men, as long as their present habits continue, *they* should be disposed to take the friendly hints here dropped, and to "consider their ways," we may all have reason to rejoice together that this labour of sincere good will has not been in vain.

It is common to remind the *young* that they occupy a station in their course peculiarly critical and important; that youth is the seed-time of life; that this is the period in which knowledge is to be acquired, habits to be formed, and provision to be made for all coming time. To young men in college all these suggestions are peculiarly appropriate. To no point of time, perhaps, in your whole course, can the epithets *critical* and *important* be so justly and strongly applied as to that which embraces your college life. Now you are first brought into anything like close contact with the world. Now your character is to be tried in a manner that it has never yet been. Now you are to be left more to yourselves than heretofore. Now it is to be seen whether your love of knowledge is so great as that you will study with diligence, when not constantly under the immediate eyes of your teachers. Hitherto you have had few associations but with the sober and orderly. Now you are to stand the test of being associated with some of a very different character. In your college course, habits in some respects new are to be formed. Various kinds of knowledge, to which you have been heretofore strangers, are to be acquired. Your characters are to receive a stamp which will, in all probability, be indelible. It is during the few years which, if your lives are spared, you are expected to spend in this institution, that it is to be seen whether you can withstand the blasts of corrupt influence with which every college, known to me, is more or less infected; whether you will have wisdom given you to appreciate the danger, and to turn away from the "instruction that causeth to err." In short, the college course of a young man who is pursuing an education, may be said to be, in a sense which belongs to no other period of equal extent—the "turning point" of his life. Here, we may almost say, everything for his weal or woe will be determined. No one can predict what any young man is to be till he is *tried*. This may be called—more than any other which either precedes or follows it—the *trying period*, on which more depends than any human arithmetic can calculate.

Can you wonder, then, my dear sons, that your father, aware of this, and recollecting it with the deepest interest, is anxious for your welfare? Can you wonder that he carries your situation every day before the throne of grace, and implores for you the protection and guidance of your father's God? Remember that, in every period of life, you need light and strength from on high, to enable you to resist temptation, and to improve the advantages under which you are placed. But you need this grace peculiarly *now*. Pray for it without ceasing. Be upon your guard against all the dangers of which I am about to warn you. Remember that you are now in a situation in which one false step may ruin you; in which yielding to the influence of one profligate companion may plunge you into embarrassments and difficulties from which you may never be able to extricate yourselves. "Watch and pray that you enter not into temptation." "Wherewith shall a young man cleanse his way? By taking heed thereto according to God's word." No one is so likely to escape the snares with which he is surrounded, as he who is impressed with a deep sense of his own weakness, and is continually seeking help from above.

Remember the purpose for which you have been placed in the institution to which you belong; to learn, not to teach; to obey, not to govern. Remember, too, that, without your own habitual and faithful efforts, your position in a college will be altogether unavailing.

Many parents, and, I fear, some youth, are apt to imagine that there is something in such an institution, which, as a matter of course, will fill the minds of pupils with knowledge, and lead to rich improvement. They seem to think that they are like open vessels sent to be filled, and that instruction may be poured into them without any agency, or even concurrence of their own. I trust this mistake never found a place in your minds; and that if it ever has in any measure, the little experience you have gained has completely banished it.

Your great object is to ascend the hill of literature and science. Now, in gaining this ascent, you cannot be carried or borne up on the shoulders of others. *You must climb it yourselves.* You must have *guides* in your arduous enterprise; and these guides may give you many directions, and furnish you with many articles of apparatus which will facilitate your ascent. But, after all, the exertion by which you climb must be your own act. The mind can be strengthened only by appropriate aliment, and habitual exercise. Gaining ideas and principles ; depositing them in the mind; digesting them, and making them our own; and thus strengthening, enlarging, and furnishing the intellectual powers,—all require incessant application and labour on our part. It was mental exercise and toil which, under God, enabled *Bacon*, and *Newton*, and *Milton* so much to rise above the mass of their fellow men. If they had made no personal efforts, but had depended on being borne up, and borne along by the strength of others, or by the native force of their own powers—they would never have reached the elevation which they gained. You are placed in circumstances highly favourable to your gaining knowledge, and in every way improving your minds; but unless you will consent to exert yourselves, and to labour diligently in this pursuit, you will gain but little. In silver and gold a man may be made rich, eminently rich, by the labour or munificence of others; but in intellectual furniture and strength, he can no more be enriched by the toil of others, than his daily food can be digested, and made to nourish him, by the mastication and the stomachs of those around him.

In the *gregarious* mode of life in which you are now placed, you will, no doubt, find both advantage and hindrance. In the colleges situated in our large cities, you know, the students do not usually lodge in public edifices, or board together in public refectories. They only come together daily at their recitations, and, when these are closed, return to their respective places of lodging. This was the case in the University of Pennsylvania, in which I was educated. When large numbers of students are placed in this situation with respect to each other, their harmonious action, and especially their efficient co-operation, are neither so constant nor so easy, as when they all board and lodge together in adjoining public edifices. In this latter plan there are some very material advantages. But there are some countervailing considerations. When students live apart, there may be much profligacy and mischief going on; but it is less concentrated and less seen. When they all live together, their movements are more prominent and noticeable; combination is more easy; they are more liable to excitement; and when excitement does spring up, it is apt to be more heated and violent. It is said, that in the University of *Aberdeen*, in Scotland, where there are two colleges, *Marischal* and *King's*, the students belonging to the one all lodge and board together; while the students of the other are distributed in different boarding-houses through the city. In the former, it is alleged, there is a more frequent occurrence of obtrusive noise and disorder; in the latter, more unbridled vice and profligacy, which never meet the public eye.

While I prefer, on the whole, having students immured together, yet I wish you to be aware that there are some perils connected with this system. You will find more vigilance and caution called for in regard to your associations, and more need of prudence to avoid being implicated in those excitements and combinations which are so apt to spring up where large numbers of human beings herd together. Recollect this. Be ever on the watch to guard against the evils, and to avail yourselves of the advantages which attend your position:—and may He who has all hearts and all events in his hands, grant you his blessing, and his unceasing guidance!

If I could admit the thought, my dear sons, that you resembled those students who are to be found in every college that I have ever seen, and some of whom, it is to be feared, belong to your own classes, I should not have the heart to write another sentence. I mean young men who have no real love of knowledge; no ambition to be distinguished for either wisdom or virtue; who have no regard for the peace and order of society; no respect or gratitude for their instructors; and who cannot be excited to either diligence or decency by even a regard to the feelings of their parents: who study as little as college discipline will allow, and who have no idea of enjoying life, or of manifesting manliness, but in idleness, dissipation, and those miserable disorders which indicate unprincipled vulgarity more than anything else. For such youth it is in vain to write or to reason. Their course cannot fail, without a miracle, to be disgraceful to themselves, and agonizing to those who love them. If I thought that you in any degree partook of this spirit, I should here lay down my pen in despair. But, indulging the hope that you love knowledge; that you cherish a spirit of generous ambition to be useful in your day, and to gratify your parents, I will go on, and pour out the fulness of a heart glowing with regard to your welfare. May God enable me to write, and you to read, in such a manner as may result in our mutual joy!

LETTER II.

OBEDIENCE TO THE LAWS.

"Sanctio justa, jubens honesta, et prohibens contraria."
BRACTON *de Legibus Angliæ.*

"Sine lege est sine ratione, modo, ordine."

MY DEAR SONS—In every college there is a system of laws, which all who enter it are, of course, bound to obey. And they are under this obligation anterior to any formal engagement to that purpose. Every ingenuous and honourable mind will perceive that he who offers himself as an inmate of any family or society, the rules of which are established and publicly known, must be understood as agreeing to those rules, and as coming under a virtual stipulation to obey them. He who comes in without intending to do this, and without actually doing it, will be considered by every honest man, not merely as a pest and a nuisance, but as forfeiting all title to the character of probity and honour. He who pleads, then, that he is under no obligation to conform to the known laws of a college of which he is a member, because he has not formally promised to do so, might just as well say, that he is at liberty, consistently with moral honesty, to violate the laws of the state, because he has never come under a public and formal engagement to obey them; which not one citizen in a thousand has ever done. How would such a plea be regarded by a judge or jury in a case of theft, fraud or perjury? We need not wait for an answer. He who should make such a plea, would, undoubtedly, be considered as a felon in spirit, if not proved to be one in act, and be driven from all decent society. I should certainly not be willing to entrust my purse with uncounted money in the hands of a student who should seriously advance such an apology for violating a college law.

Some years since, in the college to which it is your privilege to belong, every student, on his admission, was required formally to declare, that he had read and understood the laws of the institution; and that he "solemnly pledged his truth and honour to obey them." And yet, even then, there were students who laid high claims to the character of both truth and honour, who deliberately violated some of the most important of those laws, and even plumed themselves on the dexterity and success with which the violation was accomplished. And what do you think their plea then was? Why, that their engagement could not be called a voluntary one; that they had been placed in the college by the authority of their parents; that the promise to obey the laws was an indispensable formality, submission to which they could not avoid, without refusing to enter the institution, and this consideration, according to their extraordinary logic, liberated them from every bond of obedience! With just as much propriety might a witness, summoned to give testimony in a court of justice, allege that, inasmuch as the solemnity of taking an oath, prior to giving his testimony, was a formality forced upon him by the law of the land, without which he could not be permitted to appear as a witness, he was not bound to speak the truth. Every honest man would instinctively despise a youth who was capable of advancing such a plea. Such an one might hold his head high, and make the most lofty pretensions to honourable principles and conduct; but, in the estimation of all correct minds, he would be regarded as, virtually if not formally, a perjured villain. The very same plea might a judge, or a magistrate of any grade, make with regard to his oath of office. It is a *sine qua non* to his introduction to office. In this sense, the requisition may be called a compulsory one. He cannot perform a single official duty, or enjoy a single official privilege or emolument, without it. But what would you think of such an officer, if, after having taken the prescribed oath, he were to allege, that it was not binding, because he was obliged either to take it, or lose his office; and to imagine that he might break it without crime or dishonour? You would, doubtless, consider him as a scoundrel, quite as worthy of a place in the penitentiary as many of those whom his sentences had sent thither.

But I will not dwell longer on these degrading subterfuges, to which none but minds utterly destitute of all sound and honourable principle would ever think of resorting.

I trust, my dear sons, you will equally despise and abhor every plea, nay every thought, of this kind; and that you will avoid the society of every fellow student who is capable of avowing such a compound of meanness and profligacy. Every real gentleman who enters even a public hotel, will strictly conform to the rules of the establishment, which he finds suspended on the wall, or immediately quit the house. There is no medium in the view of a correct mind. I would infinitely rather find a son of mine honestly confessing his delinquency in violating a college law, and incurring the whole weight of the penalty, than disgracing himself by pleas which evince radical obliquity of moral principle. A youth of substantially pure moral sentiments and habits may be betrayed into an inadvertent violation of a statute under which he has voluntarily placed himself; but the refined Jesuitism, which would explain away a palpable obligation, and justify a virtual perjury, is ripe for almost every crime to which an inducement is presented.

But, independently of all engagements, either express or implied, to obey the laws under which you are placed, as members of a college, I would suggest some considerations in favour of obedience to them, which I am sure you will think weighty, unless your minds are more deplorably perverted by a factitious system of morals, than my affection for you will allow me to suppose. When you are tempted to violate the smallest law of the institution, let the following reflections occur to your minds, and exert that influence which I am sure they will on every enlightened and pure conscience.

1. By whom were these laws made? Not by capricious or unreasonable tyrants. Not by a body of austere, gloomy men, who had forgotten the season of their own youth, and were desirous of abridging your comforts, and of imposing upon you an unnecessary and painful yoke. Not at all. But by the trustees of the institution; by a body of enlightened, reasonable, conscientious men, who have been college students themselves; and, of course, know the feelings, the temptations, and the dangers of students:—by affectionate and faithful parents who feel tenderly for the welfare and happiness of youth; and would not lay upon a young man a single restraint which they did not know would be for his good:—by men of age, and culture, and experience, who have not only been young themselves, but who have seen for years the evils, nay the almost certain ruin, to which students are exposed by being left to their own inclinations:—by men whose feelings are predominantly kind and benevolent, and who would never vote for the enactment of any law, which had not been found by experience to be indispensable:—by men who have deliberately taken an oath to promote the best interests of the institution, and of the youth committed to their care. Surely laws formed by such men; deliberately reviewed and persisted in from year to year; and carefully modified as circumstances may require;—ought to be regarded with deep respect, and to bind the heart, as well as the conscience, of every ingenuous student. The young man who, when such laws are in question, can treat them with contempt, or even with neglect, has, indeed, little reason to plume himself upon either the

soundness of his understanding, or the rectitude of his moral feelings.

2. Reflect whether you have any just reason to find fault with any one of these laws. I do not ask, whether many disorderly and unprincipled students would not wish some of them to be repealed or altered. But is there one of them which will not stand the test of serious and impartial examination? Is there one of them unreasonable, harsh, or adapted to injure either those who are found faithfully obeying it, or any others? Is there one, concerning which you can lay your hands on your hearts, and say that it would be for the benefit of the college and of the students that it should be repealed? I am verily persuaded that the most reckless and licentious member of your college, or of any college—if he would go over the whole code of its laws in detail, and suffer his sober moral sense deliberately to sit in judgment upon each one, could not find one which he would be willing to say ought to be expunged. Let him single out from all the prohibited offences against the order of the college, that one which he should judge to involve the least degree of moral turpitude, and then ask himself what would be the consequence if that offence were habitually committed by every student in the house? This is the real test to which every matter of the kind in question ought to be brought. He who on any occasion, or in regard to any subject, allows himself to do a thing, or to act upon a principle, which, if it were made the principle of universal action, would be productive of much mischief, must be considered by all sober thinkers as an offender against the peace and order of society. Will this reasoning be deemed too refined, or too much removed from the feelings of common life to be recognized as practically important by an intelligent young man, who is beginning to feel his obligations as a patriot and a social being, if not as a Christian? I would fain hope not. There must be something radically rotten in the moral principles of that youth, who refuses to consider whether the course he is pursuing

is injurious or not to the institution with which he is connected, or to the best interests of society at large; or who deliberately resolves, at the expense of such injury, to indulge his criminal passions. Surely he need not be told, that this is the essential character of those wretched invaders of the peace of society, whom public justice pronounces unfit to go at large, or even to live.

3. Reflect further, how much it is your own interest to obey every jot and tittle of the laws under which you are placed. Need I say, that the more scrupulous and faithful your obedience to all the rules of the institution, the less of your time will be withdrawn from your studies, and wasted in plotting mischief; in adopting mean and lying contrivances to escape detection; and in that uneasiness and dissipation of thought to which scenes of disorder always lead? Many a deluded youth has forfeited his scholarship, and lost his standing in his class, by squandering those hours in plans of ingenious disobedience which he would otherwise have devoted to his studies. Remember, too, that the more exemplary your obedience to all the laws of the college, the more you will gain the esteem and confidence of your instructors, and the more favourable your prospect of obtaining that grade of honour in your class, to which your talents and acquirements may entitle you. For it must not be forgotten, that in every well regulated and faithfully conducted college, the moral conduct of every student, and his obedience to the laws, are necessarily taken into the account, in estimating his title to the honours dispensed to his class. Accordingly, I have known students of the finest talents, and of elevated attainments, to close their collegial career in the second, if not the third grade of literary rank, merely because they had been characteristically regardless of some of the laws of the institution with which they were connected; and, though often reproved for their delinquency, failed to profit by the admonitions of their teachers. Nor did any one, except, perhaps, some partial and blinded

parents, disapprove of the award. In fact, it could not have been ordered otherwise, without gross injustice to the individuals concerned, and no less injustice to the institution whose laws they had trampled under feet. Let it also be borne in mind, that he who is punctual in obeying every prescribed law, is more easy and comfortable in his own mind; approaches his teachers and his fellow-students with more fearless confidence; and is affected with none of that torturing anxiety which must ever, in a greater or less degree, invade the peace of him who is conscious of being chargeable with habitual violations of the laws which he is bound to obey. How sweet and enviable must have been the feelings of a distinguished young gentleman from the South, of fine talents and scholarship, and of a wealthy family, whom I once knew, who, after he had been a member of the college in this place for several years, was able to say, "I am not conscious of having violated the smallest law of the institution since I have been connected with it." It is hardly necessary to say, that his career was a pleasant and honourable one, and that he left the college enjoying the respect and love of all who knew him.

4. Consider, further, how much credit you will reflect on your Alma Mater by a punctual and exemplary conformity to her regulations. Travellers, in passing through Princeton, have been, more than once, prejudiced against our college, by happening to see several students hanging about the tavern doors; swaggering with an air of vulgar and insolent importance; smoking, and, perhaps, using profane language. Now, though I conscientiously believe that scenes of this kind are not so frequently exhibited in your college as in some others; yet whenever exhibited, they will not fail to prejudice some individuals who may happen to witness them. The travellers to whom I refer—not pious, but worldly-minded and gay, yet polished and reflecting, have, in some instances, to my certain knowledge, most unjustly, formed conclusions

against the college from this unfavourable specimen of its students; and have resolved never to send a son to it, lest he should be brought up in the midst of vulgarity and profaneness.

Impressions of this kind, though most unjust, have been more than once made by the appearance of a single unfortunate individual, and a general character of the college and of its inmates thence derived, of a very unfavourable kind. I need not say, that a candid and generous minded young man would be deeply pained at the thought of inflicting such a wound on the reputation of his literary mother; and that he would consider any one thus capable of sporting with the character of an individual, and much more of an important public institution, as deeply guilty.

5. Reflect, once more, on the position in which your teachers are placed with regard to the execution of the laws. Perhaps no feeling is more apt to spring up in the minds of college students, than that of hostility to their instructors. They are prone to consider the Faculty, as, of course, an adverse body, needlessly strict, and even tyrannical, and leagued against their pleasures. From this feeling, the transition is easy to the habit of regarding the faculty, in enforcing the laws, as a body which it is no sin to oppose, and over which it is rather a meritorious act to gain a triumph. Can it be necessary to employ reasoning to show that such feelings and sentiments are highly absurd; and that those who indulge them take the most preposterous ground? Are not the members of college faculties men of like passions with others? Is it reasonable to accuse them of gratuitous and wanton oppression? Can they be supposed to have an interest in making the college to which they belong unpopular, with either parents or young men, and, of course, driving students away from it? On the contrary, is it not manifestly the interest of every one, from the president down to the youngest tutor, to teach and govern in such a manner as to be acceptable to all, and to draw as many

students as possible to the institution with which he is connected? True, indeed, they have all solemnly sworn faithfully to execute the laws of the institutions, in which they are respectively placed as teachers; and if they are wise and honest men, they are fully persuaded, that carrying all the laws into execution, is the best method for securing the welfare and happiness of the pupils themselves, as well as the best interest of all concerned. Under these engagements and convictions can they be blamed for acting according to their conscientious impressions of duty? Would you not secretly despise them if they acted otherwise? How unreasonable, then, the prejudice against them for discharging a duty, which all acknowledge to be solemnly required at their hands! The truth is, instead of there being any temptation impelling the members of any faculty to be over-rigorous or oppressive in the execution of college laws, the temptation is, in almost all cases, the other way. And I am compelled to say, that, after going through a college course myself, more than fifty years ago; and after having been an attentive observer of the character, course of instruction, and discipline of different colleges for more than forty years;—I say, after all this opportunity for observation, I am constrained to assert, that I have seldom known any college faculty to err on the side of excessive rigour, in the execution of the code of laws with which they were entrusted; but that the mistake has, almost always, been on the side of undue laxity, rather than the reverse. Discipline has commonly been either too tardy in its pace, or marked with too much lenity in its character. Here has been the fruitful source of a large portion of the evils which beset bands of college students. If discipline were conducted with more strictness than it is, rather than less; if learners in our public institutions were more accustomed to "bear the yoke in their youth," it were better for them, and better for the institutions to which they belong.

I hope, my dear sons, it is not necessary for me to

say, that my object, in all that has been said, is not to make you either mopes or slaves. On the contrary, I am persuaded that the more perfectly you imbibe the spirit, and form the habits which I have recommended, the more happy; the more truly free and independent; the more manly and gentlemanly in the best sense of those words; the more highly respectable you will ever appear, in your own eyes, and in the eyes of all around you. My acquaintance with college students has been large, and somewhat intimate; and my recollection enables me unequivocally to affirm, that the most accomplished scholars, the most enlarged and independent thinkers, the most high-minded and honourable individuals of the whole number that I have ever known, were precisely those whose obedience to the laws was most perfect; who knew the value of order in conduct as well as in study; who invariably treated their instructors with respect, and enjoyed their entire confidence; who never met them but with an erect and assured countenance; and whose whole character was regarded by all their associates as elevated and honourable. Such has been my invariable experience. To imagine that the contrary is apt to be the case, is a miserable delusion. So fixed is my persuasion of the truth of this statement, that whenever I hear that a young man has fallen under the frowns and the discipline of his instructors, I take for granted, without a moment's hesitation, that he is a poor scholar, and that, however he may boast of his "honour," or his "independence," he has very little of either to spare.

Do you ask me what portions or classes of the laws I would have you studiously to obey? I answer, The whole—every "jot and tittle," from the most deeply vital to the most trivial and minute. You as really break the laws of the institution with which you are connected, and as really forfeit that "truth and honour" which you have virtually, if not formally pledged—by cutting with your penknife the fences and doors, and window casements and seats of the college, as by more bold and dangerous acts of disorder. Only suppose every one to indulge in such a propensity, and to what a disgusting and miserable state would everything in and about the college edifices be speedily reduced! But it is my wish, with peculiar emphasis, to guard you against all participation in those infractions of law, which lead to public disturbance, and especially which endanger health or life. When I have heard of students who claimed to be young "gentlemen of honour," exploding gunpowder in the college-rooms, to the destruction of property, and at the most imminent risk of personal, and perhaps fatal, injury of some fellow student or teacher, I have found it difficult to avoid the impression, not merely that the perpetrator was an unprincipled and dishonoured youth; but that he was actuated by those reckless and vile passions which distinguish the murderer; that he was wholly unfit to occupy a place in decent society; and that the state prison was his proper abode.

Say not that this language is too severe. It is the language of "truth and soberness." It is true, I should lament such an outrage, if not followed by fatal effects, less—much less than where a life had been lost. But as to the *quo animo*, it does really appear to me, that he who can deliberately lend himself to such an outrage as has been referred to, deserves little if any less abhorrence than many a midnight assassin.

I have only to add, that, where this species of outrage is so planned and conducted (as has more than once occurred in different colleges) as to invade the peace of a private family, and to fill with terror and with anguish, and expose to imminent danger, delicate females, there is a degree of brutality added to crime, of which it is not easy to speak in terms expressive of adequate abhorrence.

There appear to be strange misapprehensions of moral principle in the minds of many of the members of our literary institutions. I have known young men who would have shrunk with instinctive abhorrence from stealing private property; who would have thought themselves permanently and deeply dishonoured, by injuring the dwelling, or invading the peace of a private family; who could, at the same time, without any feeling of self-reproach or shame, take out and bear off, without permission, a book from a public library, and neglect to return it; who could break or purloin a rare and valuable piece of philosophical apparatus; deface or destroy the property of the college to which they were so much inindebted, in a manner which if it were directed against their own property, they would feel justified in prosecuting the invader to the penitentiary; and, in short, act as if, by becoming pupils in a public institution, they became, in a sort, joint partners in all the property of the institution, and entitled to treat it as in a measure their own, or with more reckless waste than they would their own. A more preposterous notion cannot be entertained by any mind. Recollect, I beseech you, that no part of the property of the college is yours. The whole of it is vested in a corporation—the board of trustees—for a great public benefit. They permit you and your fellow students to enter, and enjoy the privileges of the institution. To prepare it for your beneficial use, they have toiled and laboured much, and gone to great expense, and are daily incurring large expenditures. So far from their being debtors to you, you are deep debtors to them; and, therefore, when you injure or destroy their property, you add the gross sin of robbery to criminal ingratitude. You are guilty of a public wrong, involving, in some respects, a deeper moral turpitude than that which is of a private nature.

For my part, when I see a young man in college disorderly in his habits, disobedient to law, labouring to deceive, and vex, and outwit his instructors, and injure the property of the institution, I have scarcely ever the least hope that he will make a decent or a useful man. I have carefully watched hundreds of this character, and have rarely found my augury of their fate falsified. Such young men have generally turned out disreputable members of society—drunkards, gamblers, swindlers, duelists; and have been either in mercy to society cut off in their course, and consigned to an early grave; or spared only to be a curse to the community, and a disgrace and an anguish to all who took an interest in their welfare.

It cannot be doubted, that, on this subject, parents are oftentimes quite as much, if not more to blame than their sons, who are chargeable with violating college laws. Both parents and children, in many cases, seem to labour under the mistake, that students, and the members of the college faculty, by whom they are instructed and governed, are to be considered as standing upon an equal footing, and that their intercourse ought to be that of independent gentlemen with each other. To illustrate this fact, I would refer you to a case which not long since occurred—not, I am happy to say, in the College of New Jersey, but in one of the distant colleges in our land. Three young men were sent to the institution in question, by their respective parents. In a short time after one of them had reached the college, he violated one of the laws, and was pointedly reproved by a professor. He immediately wrote to his father that the professor had insulted him. The father promptly answered thus:—"My son, go and purchase for yourself the largest cane in the town, and break it over the professor's head." The other two wrote to their father that after having tried the college for a few weeks, they were not pleased with it, and, without any permission, had removed to another college, and had taken lodgings in the best hotel in the place! Of such young men no reasonable person would ever expect to hear any good. And it is certainly quite reasonable to add, that when such young men go to destruction, and disgrace their families, by far the largest amount of blame lies at the door of their parents.

LETTER III.

MANNERS.

Non contemnenda, tanquam parva, sine quibus magna constare non possint. JEROME.

MY DEAR SONS—It is remarked, by a good writer, that "the ancients began the education of their children by forming their hearts and manners. They taught them the duty of men, and of citizens. We teach them the languages of the ancients, and leave their morals and manners to shift for themselves." Without pausing to examine either the justice, or the proper extent of this statement, it cannot be doubted that there is a measure of truth in it. It cannot be doubted that the majority of the youth of the present day, who have been trained in literature and science, manifest less modesty, less of the becoming spirit of subordination, less respect for age, less of gentle, docile, filial deference for superiors, than were common in the days of our fathers. I trust that, in saying this, I shall not be set down as a prejudiced *laudator temporis acti;* as unreasonably yielding to the partiality of an old man for the days and habits of his youth. Fifty or sixty years ago, unless I am greatly deceived, the intercourse between the professors and tutors of our colleges and their pupils, was considerably different from what it now is. There is less of sovereign, unquestioned, parental authority on the part of the former; and much less of that implicit obedience on the part of the latter, and of those outward testimonials of respect and reverence which were then deemed indispensable. In my early days, in several of the most respectable and popular colleges in our country, no student ever entered the public edifice in which he either lodged or recited without taking off his hat: nor did he ever allow himself to come within a number of feet of any officer of the college, either within doors or in the open air, without uncovering his head. The approach of such an officer would, then, instantly command silence and perfect decorum. Is it so now? and is the alteration for the better or the worse? If there were in the old habits of some of our colleges an air of formal servility, is there not, at present, too often an air of disrespect and insolent boorishness? Surely this ought not to be so. When our country is growing every day in wealth, in literature, and certainly in some species of refinement, our youth ought to be growing in all that is calculated to distinguish and adorn intellectual and moral culture, and to exhibit them as worthy of the advantages under which they are placed.

It appears to me that many young men in college labour under an entire mistake in regard to the motives which ought to influence them in regulating their manners. They seem to think that, unless they have a sincere personal respect for the individuals or bodies with whom they are called to have intercourse, they may, without any discredit to themselves, indulge in behaviour which, in other circumstances, would be liable to the charge of rudeness. But a little reflection cannot fail of convincing any sober mind that this is a great error. For, in the first place, we are bound, upon every principle, to treat with deference and respect those who are set over us in authority, whatever may be our estimate of their personal character. Their office is worthy of respect, even if their persons be not. But, independently of this consideration, which, to every thinking mind, is conclusive, we are, in the second place, bound thus to conduct ourselves, upon the principle of self-respect. When any one treats with rudeness those whom he is bound officially to obey, he may flatter himself that he is displaying his spirit, and manifesting elevation of character; but, instead of this, he is only displaying his own vulgarity and ignorance of the world, and manifesting that he is no gentleman, whatever claim to that title he may imagine himself to possess. One of the most perfect models of good-breeding that I ever saw in my life, was accustomed to overcome the incivility of the rude, by the most entire respectfulness of manner on his part. I have known him to disarm even brutality itself, by returning the strictest politeness to the most ruffian insolence.

Let me earnestly entreat you, then, to be careful—constantly and vigilantly careful of your manners to all, but especially to three classes of persons.

1. To all the members of the faculty of the college. These gentlemen are officially set over you; and, by entering the college, you have voluntarily come under a virtual engagement to submit to their authority, and to honour their persons. The supposition is, that they are all well qualified for their office, and are personally deserving of your highest respect. But whether this be so or not, there is but one course for you—and that is, to conform to the spirit of the laws, and ever to treat them as if they were perfectly worthy of veneration, as well as obedience. He who is disrespectful to his teachers, dishonours himself more than them. If, therefore, I had no regard to anything but your own reputation, I would say, pay them unceasing and vigi lant respect. Treat them all—from the president down to the youngest tutor—with scrupulous decorum and politeness. Never accost them, or pass them, whether in the public edifice, in the campus, or in the street, without lifting, or, at least, touching the hat. Never speak to them, but with the tone and manner appropriate to one who is addressing a superior. This testimonial of respect is everywhere dictated by the most obvious sense of propriety; and is really as much

due to yourselves, as claiming to be well-bred young gentlemen, as it is to the official personage to whom it is directed. Indeed I never allow myself to enter an inhabited house, whatever may be the rank or the social position of its inmates, without taking off my hat. I should certainly expect them to do so in my own house, and I would not be behind them in politeness.

I have often been amazed to see young men, who laid claim to the title of gentlemen, enter rooms in which the president, or some other officer of college, was seated or standing, and keep on their hats until they had passed, perhaps, immediately by the chair of such officer, over the whole length of the apartment to a seat at its remote end, and there slowly remove them; sometimes after being seated themselves, and with an air as if they scarcely thought it worth while to take them off even then. I never see this without confidently taking for granted that young men who can so conduct themselves, are grossly ignorant of the world, and, whatever else may have belonged to their history, have had a very vulgar breeding. They dishonour themselves far more than they dishonour the objects of this rudeness.

I have been sometimes little less disgusted to see young men, the children of respectable parents, and who ought to have been taught better, rising, when questioned at a recitation, or an examination, and answering with an air and manner becoming those who felt themselves superior to their examiners, and who wished to testify how little respect they felt for them. Such things evince as much the lack of good breeding as of good sense; and instead of manifesting that manliness, independence, and elevation of character which are intended to be displayed, are rather disgusting testimonies of ignorance and boyish self-consequence.

Another practice, which I have observed with pain among students of college, in their recitation rooms, and in other similar situations, in the presence of their instructors, is their disrespectful mode of sitting. I mean sitting with their feet lifted up, on the top of an opposite bench or chair, and stretched out in the magisterial manner of a master among his menials, or of a boon companion lounging among his equals. No truly well bred person ever allows himself to sit in this manner in the presence of his superiors, or even of his equals, unless they are his daily and hourly associates. Would not any young man, who had enjoyed a training above the grossly vulgar, be shocked to see an attitude of this kind assumed by any one in a decent circle in a parlour? Surely in the presence of his official superiors he ought to be quite as particular. I lay claim to no special delicacy or refinement in my early training; but truth requires me to say, that, such as it was, if I had been ever seen to sit in the presence of my parents, or of any decent company, as I have often seen members of college sitting in the presence of their instructors, I should have met with a prompt and severe rebuke.

Imagine to yourselves the deportment which you ought ever to exhibit toward beloved and venerated parents, in yielding prompt obedience to all their commands, and showing by every word, and look, and tone, and gesture, that you wished to treat them with perfect respect; picture to yourselves this deportment, and you have the model of that which I earnestly desire my sons ever to display toward their official instructors. In giving this counsel, as I remarked in a preceding letter, you cannot suspect me of a desire to cultivate in my children a spirit of servility; on the contrary, my earnest desire is, that they should ever cultivate those manly and elevated sentiments which evince true magnanimity of spirit, and prepare for the most honourable course of action. And, truly, you were never more mistaken, if you suppose that the manifestation of perfect reverence and docility toward your instructors, indicates any other than a spirit of real dignity and independence. Here the path of perfect obedience is the only path to perfect freedom and honour.

It is, perhaps, as proper to notice under this head, as anywhere else, a piece of ill manners which I have seen displayed in a certain collegiate institution, to my great disgust and annoyance. I mean the exhibition of a cigar in the mouth of a student in a public procession, while he was puffing his smoke in the face of all who approached or passed him. There is such a concentration of vulgarity and offensiveness in this thing, that I know not how to speak of it in terms of adequate reprobation. Few practices are more frequently connected with rustic and disagreeable manners, and offensive habits of various kinds, than the use of tobacco in any way. But to see a student sporting a cigar in a college procession, argues such a total want of decorum and refinement, as ought never to be seen in civilized society. Indeed, such an exhibition is an outrage on good manners, that I should be ashamed to speak of, had I not with my own eyes seen it—not in a public street or campus merely, but in one of the entries of a college edifice, and that on an occasion on which I was not a little mortified, that so many strangers should have an opportunity of seeing a fact so disreputable to the state of manners in a literary institution.

Of the various habits commonly connected with the free use of tobacco one ought not to pass unnoticed here, when speaking of good manners. I refer particularly to the vulgar and disgusting practice of spitting profusely on the floors around the offender, and running the risk of bespattering every individual in his neighbourhood. I have known young men in the apartments of a college, when I was sitting beside them, smell so strongly of tobacco smoke as to be scarcely endurable, and at the same time squirting their tobacco juice around them in such quantities, and with so little delicacy, that I had no alternative but either to change my seat, or to have my stomach turned. I preferred the former. But how shameful for any one who calls himself a gentleman to subject those who approach him to so severe a tax!

The truth is, when I see a student parading the streets with a cigar in his mouth, and manifesting a devoted attachment to the use of tobacco, I am pretty much in the habit of giving up all hope of his future respectability and honour. I consider him as the slave of an indulgence, which I have seen betray so many into the most degrading intemperance, and so many others into incurable ill health, that I cannot help regarding the devotee to this practice as eminently in danger of being lost to all that is honourable and good. But more of this hereafter.

2. Be attentive to your manners in all your intercourse with your fellow students. No one can depend on his deportment being such as it ought to be on special occasions, when he meets his superiors, unless he is careful to form correct habits in this respect, in his intercourse with all. Hence wise counsellors tell us, that if we desire to succeed in making healthful and graceful postures natural to us, we must take care to maintain them in our private apartments, and in our habitual and every-day attitudes. Not only on this account, but also for the purpose of promoting pleasant and profitable intercourse with your fellow students, I would earnestly exhort you to be pointedly attentive to your manners, even amidst all the unceremonious freedom of daily and hourly communication with your equals. It would, indeed, border on the ridiculous, in intercourse with fellow students, to adhere to all the punctilious forms of etiquette, which ought to be observed in regard to strangers and superiors; but still, even with class-mates and room-mates, there may be unwise freedoms, and disgusting coarseness, which ought to be carefully avoided by all who would derive the greatest advantage from the society of their fellows.

In framing a general code of manners for regulating intercourse with fellow students, the great difficulty is to avoid such details as would be tedious, and at the same time to go into particulars sufficiently to furnish an adequate guide for most practical occasions. I shall endeavour to pursue such a middle course as to make my counsels intelligible, and adapted to the occurrences of every day, without being unduly minute.

Remember, then, if you desire to be regarded by every fellow student with good will and respect, to avoid everything that is adapted to wound or irritate feelings. The language of ridicule, of sneer, of sarcasm, of harsh censure, can never be uttered, even to your most intimate companion, without producing more or less alienation. A rough tone, a contemptuous look, a disrespectful epithet or insinuation, seldom fails to leave an impression, which, though not openly resented at the moment, is not easily effaced. I have known such impressions to last for years, and him who received them to complain, that, though retaining them was contrary to his own better judgment, he was unable to dismiss them from his mind. If a fellow student be of such a temper or character that you wish to avoid all intercourse with him, let not your deportment, unless in very extreme and extraordinary cases, be that of haughty contempt, of scorn, or of open reproach, which might naturally lead to collision and violence; a collision and violence always to be deprecated in proportion to the evil character of the individual desired to be avoided. Many a youth, under the impulse of a generous and high-minded abhorrence of vice, has inconsiderately testified that abhorrence in a way which has unnecessarily drawn upon him the bitter resentment and brutal violence of a ruffian, which might easily have been avoided without any unfaithfulness to the cause of virtue. The aim of a young person, to avoid giving countenance to vice, may be much more appropriately and happily gained, by a deportment of dignified reserve, of quiet and silent but firm withdrawment from all communication.

But in regard to those fellow students who do not, by either folly or vice, render all comfortable intercourse with them impracticable, make a point of maintaining, toward them all, a deportment respectful, kind, and conciliatory. You will, of course, be more intimate with some than with others. Nay, I would strongly advise you to be really intimate with very few. But for such intimacy I hope you will not fail to select the best scholars, and the most polished, pure, and honourable of the whole number; those whose talents and acquirements will render their society profitable, and whose moral correctness will render them safe associates. But while you do this, try to establish, with all, the character of perfect gentlemen, and young men of strict honour. Avoid all lofty airs; all repulsive looks, gestures, and language in addressing them. Be ready to oblige, affable and accommodating to every one. You will find a number of students in the college, and perhaps some among your classmates, whose parents are known to be in straitened circumstances, and who manifest by their strict economy, their plain dress, and by all their habits, that they are poor. Let me charge you never to be guilty of the weakness of undervaluing such, merely on account of their poverty, and preferring to associate with the children of the rich, merely on account of their fancied superior rank. There is a littleness and a folly in such estimates, of which I hope my children will never be guilty. Respect and treat every student according to his personal worth, not according to his purse. Recollect that, a few years hence, the youth, the scantiness of whose finances kept him modest and sober-minded, may be found to have far outstripped in learning, in wisdom, in virtue, and true elevation in society, the son of the proudest nabob, who, on account of his well-lined pocket, proved a miserable scholar, and an ignoble profligate.

3. I have only to add, that it is of more importance than is commonly supposed, for college students to maintain becoming manners toward the inhabitants of the town when called to have intercourse with them.

The readiness of college students to quarrel with the townspeople in the midst of whom they live, is an old occurrence, to which there is a continual tendency, and of which the consequences are as mischievous as they are painful. The pride and folly of students are apt to take the alarm where no insult or injury was intended; and the morbid and ridiculous sensibility of townspeople frequently leads them seriously to resent that which ought to have been overlooked as an effusion of childish weakness. In how many instances has this miserable folly led to conflicts and violence, of which all parties had reason to be ashamed!

My desire, my dear sons, and my earnest advice is, that in moving about through the village in which your college is placed, and in all your occasional intercourse with its inhabitants, you manifest all the decorum and delicacy of young gentlemen, who have too much self-respect to violate the feelings of others; and too much regard to what is due to every fellow-creature to allow of your indulging caprice, or selfishness, or ill-humour, at their expense. When you pass either boys or adults in the street, let no indication of either contempt or hostile feeling escape you. If any feeling of that kind is manifested on their part, do not permit yourselves, in ordinary circumstances, to understand or to notice it. Instead of its being manly to resent, or to chastise the petty insolence of such people, it is rather the part of wayward children, who, by such conduct, expose their own weakness and ignorance of the world, rather than the ill conduct of others. I have never known a fracas to occur, as it is commonly expressed, between college students and town-boys, however ill the latter may have behaved, without finding occasion to throw nine-tenths of the blame on the former. Young men of cultivated minds and polished habits ought to have too much discernment, and too much consideration, to plunge headlong into a conflict from which neither credit nor profit can possibly be derived; from which, even if they are victorious, nothing but disgrace can result. What though town-boys adopt the opinion, that the students of college are unwilling to fight with them? What though they think and say, that they are either too proud or too cowardly to enter the lists with them? What harm can such imputations do you? Is it not better to bear them in silence, when it is evident that your character cannot be materially affected by them, than to engage in a contest of fisticuffs with those who are reckless of consequences; to be rolled in the dust; to have your garments torn from your backs; and to retire from the contest with black eyes, and bloody noses, and perhaps the loss of limb, or even life to some; and after all, with the miserable consolation that you have finally gained a victory, from which no honour can possibly be derived, but, on the contrary, it may be, many a painful memorial lasting as life?

If you desire wholly to avoid such dishonourable conflicts, you must carefully avoid everything which can possibly lead to them. "The prudent man," says Solomon, "foreseeth the evil and hideth himself, but the simple pass on and are punished." A very small amount of discretion will be sufficient to put you on your guard against all those modes of treating the people of the town, whether young or old, which will be apt to draw upon you their dislike, or excite them to particular acts of personal disrespect or violence. Whether you enter the store of the merchant, the shop of the mechanic, or the hotel of the publican; whether you encounter the townsman in the social circle, or his children or apprentices in the street, let nothing approaching to the offensive escape you toward any of them. If any mechanic should either do your work badly, or overreach you in his charges, or in any way treat you ill, I hope you will never think of quarrelling with him, or assailing him with abusive language; but simply of withdrawing from him, and never again putting yourselves in his power. And so if any word, or look, or gesture of insolent character should be shown by any of the townspeople, young or old, do not appear to notice it. Turn away, and try to avoid coming in contact with them again. Reject with scorn, as a dictate at once of sin and folly, the maxim so often in the mouth of youthful inexperience—"that it is dastardly to take an uncivil word or look from any one without resenting it." He who acts upon this maxim may always expect to have a sufficient number of quarrels and broils on his hands; and, in fact, to be at the mercy of every ruffian who wishes to involve him in a disreputable conflict.

I have sometimes seen young men in "Nassau Hall," whose manners in all the respects which I have mentioned, were worthy of being regarded as a model for your imitation. I wish it were in my power to hold them up to your view, with all the bright and graphic clearness with which their personal deportment was invested. I will try to set before you the example of one of their number, which will never be effaced from my memory, and which I could wish might be indelibly impressed upon yours.

The youth to whom I refer, was the son of respectable parents, in very moderate, and indeed rather straitened circumstances. He was, of course, altogether unable to indulge in large expenditures, and was obliged to exercise the strictest economy in dress, and in all his habits. He was not at all distinguished as a genius, but he had a good mind; was indefatigably diligent in study; was a good scholar, and maintained an honourable standing in his class. But his deportment as a member of the college, was above all praise. Though he was no way related to me, yet I had much opportunity of being acquainted with his character and course. And I never heard of his infringing the smallest law of the institution, or incurring the remotest frown from any member of the faculty. Whether in the lecture-room or the prayer-hall, in the refectory or the campus, his manners were those of the perfect gentleman. He was no tale-bearer. He was no supercilious censor. The strictest integrity, delicacy and honour were manifest in all his intercourse. The law of kindness and of respectfulness ever dwelt upon his tongue, and marked all his deportment. A profane or uncivil word, during the whole three years that he spent in Princeton, was, probably, never heard to escape from his lips. All his fellow students loved him; for I doubt whether, in his treatment of any one of them, he ever departed from the most perfect urbanity. He was never heard to call any of them by an offensive nickname. He never allowed himself to refer to events or circumstances adapted to give any one pain. His deportment toward the very servants of the college, was always such as to conciliate their respect, and even their affection. He was at the greatest remove from being chargeable with smiling on vice; and yet his opposition to it was maintained, rather by standing aloof from the vicious, and refraining from all fellowship with the works of darkness, than by positive reproof, or acrimonious censure. Even those whose company he avoided never complained of his deportment as uncivil. It was marked by no offensive demeanour, but by mere abstinence from their society.. The very worst of his fellow-students respected him, and "had no evil thing to say of him;" and when engaged in schemes of mischief, were almost as anxious to conceal them from him as from the members of the faculty. It is hardly necessary to add, that during his whole course in the institution, he was never once involved in a scrape or quarrel with an associate, or gave any one even a pretext for assailing him.

When this exemplary young man moved about among the people of the town, the same inoffensive and perfectly popular manners marked all his conduct. His treatment of every mechanic whom he employed; of every servant who waited on him, or accosted him; of every child in the street, was ever so distinguished by kindness and affability, that he was a favourite among them all. He was so far from ever involving himself in broils or disputes with the rudest of their number, that his approach seemed to be greeted with pleasure wherever he went. When he came to be graduated, his place on the list of honours was quite as high as he deserved, because everybody loved and delighted to do him honour. And when he returned to the village, from time to time, for a number of years after he had left it, he was hailed by all, from the highest to the lowest, as a respected friend.

If I could cherish the hope, my dear sons, that you would walk in the steps of this admirable youth, and leave the institution with which it is your privilege to be connected, with a character like his, my highest wishes, as to this point, would be gratified. And why may you not? Are you not sensible that the manners which I have described, are precisely those which would carry you through life with popularity and honour? And do you not know that, if you wish to attain such manners, you cannot begin too early to cultivate them; and that those which you carry with you from college will be apt to follow you through life?

I have as yet said nothing of the use of profane language in common conversation, as belonging to the subject of manners. As you have been taught, from your childhood, to abhor the language of profaneness, as a sin against God, I trust there is no need of my enlarging on this point. But I wish you to remember that, independently of the offence against the Majesty of heaven, which ought to be and will be decisive with every mind not thoroughly impious, the use of such language is as gross an offence against good breeding as it is against the law of God. There is no principle of good manners more self-evident, or more generally admitted than this, that in social intercourse we ought to avoid everything adapted to give pain to those with whom we converse. Now, can it be doubted that there are many, very many with whom we are called daily to converse, who are sincerely grieved, nay, offended when they hear "the name of God taken in vain," or any form of profane speech indulged in their presence? Their sense of propriety is outraged, and their moral feelings painfully invaded by every expression of this nature. Is it the part of a gentleman to allow himself to do this? I apprehend that every man of common sense and common decency will emphatically say, No. And yet how strange is it that many, who would be astonished and offended to hear their claim to the character of gentlemen called in question, at the same time, do not scruple every day to wound the feelings of those with whom they converse, with language which, if it be not grossly blasphemous, is such as is adapted to give pain to the pious, if not to the decently moral hearer.

If these sentiments be just, what shall be said of that young man who, when he sees a clergyman, or other well known professor of religion, approaching him, within a few feet, or immediately after having passed him a similar distance, is heard to blurt out so loudly as to insure its being audible, the most profane or otherwise indecent language? This is not merely impious—it is brutal; and those who can be guilty of it, ought to be abhorred as well as despised.

The practice which I have sometimes known to be indulged in colleges, of turning particular students into ridicule, by repeating disrespectful nicknames, or by satirizing certain peculiarities or characteristics, is certainly an infringement of those good manners which ought to be cultivated in every literary institution. Suppose a gentleman in common life were called upon to be frequently in the company of a respectable Jew, or a person who had lost an eye, or who, on account of lameness, moved about on crutches, what would be thought of him, if he were continually to address these persons respectively by nicknames, reminding each of his peculiarity? Suppose he were always to call the first, whenever he spoke to him, "Israelite;" the second, "Blinkard;" and the third, "Crutch;" would he be considered as a man of good manners? Yet an offence against good manners in this respect is one of the most common faults in all the colleges I have ever known. I once knew a respectable and promising young Jew, who entered one of our colleges. His talents were good, his temper amiable, and his manners of the most inoffensive kind. Yet he was so continually twitted by a few—I am happy to say it was by a very few, of the coarse, vulgar young men around him—by various forms of ridicule, that the residence of a few weeks convinced him that he could not longer remain with comfort a member of the institution. He was withdrawn; and was prevented from ever passing through any college. How disgraceful as well as injurious is such conduct on the part of young men, estimating the value of, and seeking to obtain, a liberal education, and claiming the character of gentlemen!

And must all the principles of decorum and delicacy be set aside for the sake of giving leave to coarse young men, whenever an unfortunate companion approaches them, to remind him of his infirmity by a ludicrous or contemptuous nickname? It would be outrageous in the walks of decent life. Ought it to be deemed otherwise in college life, where decorum and refinement ought to hold a sacred reign?

My dear sons, there is more, after all, in the efficacy of manners, than I can tell you in one short letter. If it be true, as has been sometimes said, that "a good face is an open letter of recommendation," it is equally true that there is a magic in pleasant manners, which scarcely anything can resist. They can cover a multitude of defects; and they have a thousand times done more for men than all their substantial qualities put together. The youth who undervalues or neglects them, whatever other advantages he may possess, is under a miserable delusion.

I have dwelt so long on this subject that I fear you will begin to think it an intricate one, and imagine that tolerable skill in this matter will be of difficult attainment. If this be the case you greatly mistake. I grant, indeed, that the conventional habits of courtly society are not to be acquired at once by the inexperienced youth. Much intercourse with the polite world and close observation are indispensable to familiarity and skill in these matters. But the cultivation and attainment of those manners for which I now plead, is a simple and easy thing. Let the most youthful student who can be expected to be found within the walls of a college, only possess good sense, true benevolence, and, of course, an unwillingness to give pain to any one, and a sincere desire to make all around him happy; let him be affable, good-tempered, and desirous of pleasing all around him. Suppose him to possess these simple elements of moral character, and nothing more will be necessary to make him an inoffensive and pleasant companion in a literary institution, or in any part of the world.

LETTER IV.

MORALS.

"Qui proficit in literis, et deficit in moribus, non proficit, sed deficit." OECOLAMPADIUS.

"The excesses of our youth are drafts upon our old age, payable, with interest, about thirty years after date." LACON I. 76.

MY DEAR SONS—The disposition to prefer intellectual to moral reputation is deplorably prevalent in seminaries of learning. Many an ambitious youth, if he could establish a character for distinguished genius and scholarship, would be quite content to lie under the imputation of moral delinquency. Or, at least, if he must be defective in either, he would decisively choose that it should be in regard to moral purity. I need not say, that this preference is an instance of deplorable infatuation. It is as much opposed to common sense as it is to the word of God. And it is of the utmost importance that the minds of youth be early imbued with sentiments adapted to its correction.

I am aware that many sober thinkers are opposed to the consideration of this subject apart from religion. They insist that what is called moral philosophy, is a mere system of refined infidelity; that pure morals cannot be hoped for, and ought not to be inculcated, apart from pure, evangelical religion; and that all attempts to promote them on any other principles, is an attempt to "gather grapes of thorns and figs of thistles." I am by no means able to concur in this opinion, especially in all its extent. I acknowledge, indeed, that the Bible is the only infallible and perfectly pure teacher of morals. I acknowledge, too, that nothing can be relied on, either for the attainment or the maintenance of sound morality, but the religion of Jesus Christ, sincerely believed and embraced as a practical system. He who expects strict moral principle to hold a consistent and steady reign in the heart of any man who is not a real Christian, will infallibly be disappointed. Yet I should not be willing to say, that duty ought in no case to be inculcated by any other arguments than those drawn from the gospel. I should more than hesitate to assert, that lying, and theft, and fraud, and drunkenness, and impurity, and gambling ought never to be prohibited by reasonings which the infidel might not be made to feel, as well as the Christian. These sins, indeed, ought always to be denounced as forbidden in the word of God; as objects of his righteous displeasure; as contrary to the spirit and will of Christ; and as wholly inconsistent with the Christian character. But may they not—ought they not to be made to appear vile and hateful, even in the eyes of the sceptic and atheist? Is it wrong to tell men that there are crimes against the community, as well as against God; that the practice of them is unreasonable, injurious to all the interests of the individual and of society, unfriendly to health, to peace of mind, to the principles of justice, benevolence and truth; in short, to hold up to view their mischievous and odious character by representations, which the rejecter of revelation, no less than the professed believer, will see to be conclusive? The moral philosopher may indeed be an infidel. When he is so, it is to be deplored. He is shorn of a large part of his strength. Still he has a number of weapons left, which are not without their value and their convincing power, even to a brother in unbelief. He may, with great propriety, tell those who listen to him, that the crimes above specified are hurtful to himself, to his intellect, to his physical frame, to his reputation, to his influence in society, to his children, to the community at large. This is moral philosophy. Its best armoury, no doubt, is the Bible; but, at the same time, it is not without weapons which those who reject the Bible may feel and be benefited by.

The object of this letter, my dear sons, is to convince you that good morals are indispensable to the safety, health, happiness, and true welfare of all, in every walk of life; and, therefore, that those who are preparing to live by the acquirement of an education, and by professional character, ought to make their moral culture an object of primary and unceasing attention. A man without genius, without eminent talents, may be both useful and happy. With barely decent powers of mind, if he be honest, sober, industrious, and prudent, he may be beloved, respected and highly useful; may "serve his generation by the will of God," and leave a name behind him of unspeakably more value than great riches. But however transcendent his talents, if he be a liar, intemperate, dishonest, or licentious, he will, of course, be despised by the wise and the good, and no degree of patronage can give him an honourable standing in society. In fact, no one without a fair moral character can hope to rise in the world; and the more firm and fixed that character, the more precious a treasure it will be found, whatever may be our lot in life.

Need I tell you, for example, how fatal intemperance is to the body, to the mind, to reputation, to all professional respectability and success? Need I attempt to set before you the melancholy picture, so often presented to the public view, of talents degraded, of health undermined and ruined, of property squandered, of families prostrated by this fell destroyer? Who that has seen so many of the deplorable triumphs of strong drink over all the best interests of man for time and eternity, can hold his peace, or forbear to proclaim to every young man, "Fly,—O fly from this arch-foe to human happiness! Let nothing tempt you to touch or taste the fatal cup. There is death in it. Your only safety is in total abstinence from the stimulus of strong drink in every form. If you allow yourself to taste it at all, there is too much reason to fear that it will become your master, and prove your ruin." When I hear of a young man that he has a fondness for strong drink, and has been seen under the power of intoxication, I instinctively give him up as lost, and abandon all hope of ever seeing him either respectable or useful. There is no sin which more directly tends to secure its own continuance and increase, or which more infallibly produces the wreck of all human prosperity. What though the deluded youth intends only to indulge to a small extent, and to avoid habitual excess? What though he abhors the character of the drunkard, and is firmly determined to stop long before he reaches the drunkard's dishonour? Does he not know that there is not the least reason to rely upon his own resolution, however sincere at the time, and that he who parleys with the tempter is probably lost?

No less fatal to the true honour and happiness of a young man is the want of integrity. What though he had all the talents and all the scholarship that ever fell to the lot of a mortal? Yet if he were known to be regardless of truth, to be destitute of honesty and honour in the intercourse of society,—who would respect him? who could avoid instinctively despising him? Who would think of employing or trusting him in matters of weight and importance? Even the worst of his classmates would turn away from him with contempt and abhorrence, as unworthy of confidence in anything. And in regard to his future profession and prospects, what could be more hopeless? It cannot be supposed that such a young man would seek the office of a minister of the gospel; from that the common consent of all would, of course, exclude him. But what other profession could he safely or honourably fill? None. In none could he obtain public esteem. In none could he succeed, either as to emolument or confidence. A sort of honour even among thieves is indispensable to that standing with his comrades, which even the occupant of such a wretched position desires to maintain.

Nothing is more directly adapted to secure to any young man the highest respect and honour among his companions, than an established character for invincible veracity; a reputation for integrity, honour, and faithfulness, which nothing can shake, nothing assail. I have known students, by no means remarkable for either talents or scholarship, who, on account of these qualities, enjoyed the esteem and confidence of their fellows to a most enviable degree; who were always selected where delicate and confidential services were to be performed; and who were remembered to the close of life for this proverbial candour and truth. My dear sons, let me have the pleasure of knowing that you sustain such a character among your classmates and companions; that the mention of your name is a pledge, with all who know you, that you would rather die than be found guilty of prevarication or falsehood in the minutest matter.

The same deplorable results must ensue to that youth, who allows himself in college to imbibe the spirit and form the habits of a gambler. The foundation of this vice is often laid within the college walls; and I need not say that there is scarcely any vice more directly adapted to "take away the heart," to fascinate the mind, to engross the attention, and to destroy him who yields to it, for both worlds. Like many other vices it begins on a small scale. The youthful votary never dreams in the outset, of going far, or adventuring much. But the fascination and the fever gradually gain upon him. From one step to another he is led on, until ruin, despair, and perhaps suicide, close his career.

Further; the use of profane language may be numbered among those immoral practices which disgrace literary institutions, and exert a mischievous influence wherever indulged. God has forbidden us to take his holy name in vain, and has declared that he "will not hold him guiltless" who violates this command. Now, we may be always said to take the name of God in vain when we pronounce it in a light and irreverent manner, and, above all, when profane oaths and imprecations, and the language of blasphemy, escape our lips. This sin is invested with so many hateful characteristics, that it is truly wonderful that any one who lays claim to culture or decency should ever be heard to indulge it. It marks a spirit of high-handed impiety. It tends to excite and encourage a similar spirit in others. It is deeply offensive and grievous to all who fear God, and reverence his word; and is, of course, a species of ill manners of the most vulgar character, of which every one who professes to be a gentleman ought to be deeply ashamed. Surely such language ought to be left to those who not only despise God and his law, but who also set at naught all that decorum which marks the intercourse of the well educated and polished portion of the community.

I shall only notice particularly one more vice, which has been the source of more injury and degradation to promising young men, than any statements or estimate of mine can adequately portray. I mean the licentiousness of the libertine in regard to the other sex. It is not easy to speak of this subject without such an offence against delicacy as is revolting to virtuous minds. Still truth must be stated, and warning given to those who have not closed their ears against all the dictates of wisdom. There is no doubt that the illicit intercourse of the sexes is the source of immeasurable misery, shame and ruin; not merely to females, destroyed by seducers, but also to the seducers themselves, and to all who are involved in their destiny. However lightly this sin may be considered by the licentious, unprincipled young man, there is, perhaps, no sin connected with more multiform and deplorable evils. It is not only a violation of the holy law of God, which denounces against it his wrath and curse, but it is productive of countless miseries in the present life of the most awful kind. It pollutes the mind. It hardens the heart. It corrupts the whole moral character. It inflicts on society heavy and complicated injuries. It destroys the peace of families. It entails infamy and misery on posterity. I have known a number of young men, otherwise of high promise, who, by a single unhallowed connection of this kind, have drawn a dark cloud over all their subsequent course; have found themselves embarrassed and depressed at every attempt to gain a respectable place in society; entirely cut off from the associations and the honours which they might otherwise have gained; and avoided by all decent people—and especially by those who have regular and orderly families, as persons whose touch is pollution.

I would say, then, to you, my sons, and to every youth in whom I felt a special interest, Turn away from this sin, and from everything which leads to it, as you would from a cup of poison, or from the assassin's dagger. If you desire to avoid becoming its victims, never allow yourselves to parley with, but fly from it. Here he who deliberates is lost. One transgression, as in the case of the drunkard's cup, may lead to another, and another, until the chains of iniquity are riveted around you, and the destruction of your character, and of all your prospects in life, is for ever sealed. If you wish to avoid the entanglements and disgrace which have entailed infamy and misery on thousands; if you would preserve a character unspotted, and do nothing to interfere with your enjoyment of that pure and happy conjugal connection, which it ought to be the desire and sacred ambition of every young man to form, as one of the noblest institutions of heaven, and, like the sabbath and the gospel, adapted to shed countless blessings on individuals and the world;—then keep yourselves pure from this sin, and sacredly avoid everything which may serve as an incentive to so great an evil.

But I will not multiply particulars further. I hope

you are convinced, my dear sons, that every form of immorality is as unfriendly to your temporal success in life, as it is offensive in the eyes of a holy God, and adapted to draw down his judgments upon you. "The way of transgressors is indeed hard." Misery and shame are its native and necessary consequences. You may hope by the force of your talents, and by the fame of your scholarship, to obviate these consequences. But this is "fighting against God." If you indulge in any form of immorality, it would require a constant course of miracles to save you from the temporal as well as eternal penalty, which a holy God has annexed to the transgression of his law. And remember, I entreat you, two things which are worthy of your serious consideration in regard to immoral practices.

The first is, that the young are peculiarly exposed to these criminal and mischievous indulgences. Their passions are strong; their experience is small; their moral principles are too often weak and wavering; their feelings are sanguine and buoyant; their self-confidence is great; and they are frequently led on by the social principle to practices which, however manifestly perilous, have never been duly considered. O how often are young persons led, "like an ox to the slaughter," by evil passions, or evil companions, or both, into habits from which they apprehend no danger! Our corrupt hearts, indeed, are apt, at all ages, to triumph over conscience and the dictates of virtue; but in youth many of the safeguards against vice, which longer experience and more sedate feelings furnish, either do not exist at all, or operate much more feebly. O, if a young man, when he begins to slide, could see, as his older friends or his parents see, the yawning gulf on the brink of which he stands, and the awful peril to which he is exposed, he would be thankful to any one who should interpose, and with a friendly hand forcibly pull him away from the precipice. But as he is peculiarly exposed to danger, so it is hard to make him see or feel its reality.

The second consideration worthy of your serious regard is, that as youth is a season of peculiar exposure to the entanglements of immorality, so the immoral habits then formed are peculiarly apt to establish a fatal reign, and finally and totally to destroy their unhappy victims. Habits formed in the morning of life are apt to "grow with the growth, and strengthen with the strength." It has been remarked by sagacious observers of human nature, that as young men, from the ardour of their feelings, and their love of excitement, are more apt, for example, to be ensnared by strong drink than those more advanced in life; so tippling habits formed in early life are peculiarly apt to gain strength, to take a firmer and more morbid hold of the physical frame, and to drag their victim more powerfully and speedily to a drunkard's grave.

The same general remark may be made concerning almost every other form of vice;—concerning departures from the solemnity of truth, the indulgence of illicit sexual intercourse, and approaches to the gambler's career. He who is enabled to keep himself pure from these sins during his youth, has gained an advantage, for which he can never be sufficiently thankful. Every successive year that this happy exemption continues, augments, under God, his ground of confidence and hope. Now is the time, my dear sons, if you wish to form habits which will bear reflection; which will secure you from the vices which are daily destroying thousands; which will prepare you, by the blessing of God, for a useful and honoured career; and for a green and happy old age, with bodily and mental faculties unimpaired by excess; with grateful recollections of the past, and with a good hope through grace for the future. Guard with the utmost care, and with humble, unceasing application to the God of all grace for strength, against every approach to that which is forbidden. And remember that in all the extent of the expression it may be said, that "the ways of wisdom are ways of pleasantness, and all her paths peace."

LETTER V.

RELIGION.

Chose admirable! la religion Chrêtienne, qui ne semble avoir d'objet que la félicité de l'autre vie, fait encore nôtre bonheur dans celle-ci.
MONTESQUIEU.

MY DEAR SONS—I have hitherto addressed you on subjects so practically and immediately important in college life; so universally acknowledged to be essential to all decorum of character, and all respectability of standing in decent society, that you will not, it is presumed, admit for a moment of doubt or cavil in regard to anything which has been advanced. But I must now request your attention to a subject, concerning which there is great diversity of opinion, and especially of feeling, among young men. For though it is, incontrovertibly, the most important of all subjects which the human mind can contemplate; yet you see and hear enough every day to know, that the great majority of those around you, of all ages, and especially of those who are borne along by the sanguine hopes and the ardent passions of youth, have no disposition to make religion even an object of serious inquiry, much less to submit to its governing power. Yet can anything be more self-evident than that, if there be an object within the range of human study more worthy of supreme attention than all others, religion is that object? Surely, to every thinking being, the existence and character of our Almighty Creator; the relations and responsibility which we bear to him; the means of obtaining his favour; the immortality and destiny of our souls; and the method of securing endless blessedness, when all the possessions and enjoyments of this world shall have passed away—are objects of regard which infinitely transcend all others in interest and importance. How, then, shall we account for the undeniable fact, that these great objects, though confessedly the most interesting that can be presented to the human mind, are precisely those which educated, intellectual young men are more apt to neglect and disregard than all others? I can account for this unquestionable and distressing fact, only by recognizing as assuredly true, what the Bible declares concerning our fallen and depraved nature;—that "the natural (or unrenewed) man receiveth not the things of the Spirit of God, neither can he know them, because they are spiritually discerned;"—that "madness is in the hearts of men while they live, and after that they go to the dead." This statement solves the difficulty; and shows us why it is that, while a great majority, even of the young, grant in words that piety is both wisdom and happiness; while they confess that they ought to be pious; and while so many profess to lament that they are not pious; yet that millions with these confessions on their lips, voluntarily neglect this great concern, as if it were known to be the veriest fable. Their judgments are in favour of it. Their consciences tell them that it ought not to be neglected; but "they have no heart for it;" and hence they go on from day to day to postpone all attention to it, without anxiety, and without regret.

Allow me to hope that my beloved sons—who have been dedicated to God in holy baptism; who have lived, from their infancy, in a house of Bibles, and of prayer; and who have already seen, even in the few years they have lived, so many of the deplorable fruits of impiety—will not indulge in this infatuation; or rather, that they will beg of the God of all grace to enable them to take a wiser course, and, like one commended of old, to choose that good part which shall not be taken away from them.

But where, on this subject, shall I begin? That every human being has within him an immortal spirit which will survive the dissolution of the body; that there is a God who made us, who has a right to our services, and who will finally be our judge; that he is a being of infinite holiness, who cannot look upon sin but with abhorrence; and that without his favour we can never be happy—these are first principles on this great subject, which, it is presumed, no one but an atheist will, for a moment, deny or question. But how the favour of this great Being, with all its precious results, is to be obtained, and our happiness in both worlds secured, is the grand question which religion—the religion of Jesus Christ, and that alone, can satisfactorily answer.

The great principle with which we are to begin, in all our inquiries on this subject, is that we are sinners; that we need pardon for our offences, and the purification of our depraved nature. No expressions are more common among all classes of men than those of Saviour and salvation. But why do we need a Saviour, unless we are involved in guilt and ruin before God? Why need a Redeemer and redemption, unless we are the bond slaves of sin and Satan, and can be ransomed only by an Almighty Deliverer, paying our debt to the justice of God, and making an atonement for our sins? Accordingly the word of God teaches us, not merely that, if we go on to forget and neglect the divine law, we are in danger of incurring the awful displeasure of our Maker and Sovereign, but that we are "condemned already;" that we are by nature guilty and polluted, and must inevitably perish, unless we are delivered from condemnation and depravity by the power and grace of the Saviour. The whole strain of Scripture, from beginning to end, represents us as in these deplorable circumstances. When it proclaims that Christ came "to seek and to save the lost;" when it tells us that "the whole have no need of a physician, but they who are sick;" when it calls upon all the children of men in every situation of life to "repent of sin;" and when it assures us that, without a renovation of our nature, we can never see the face of God in peace, it is evident that all these representations conspire to fasten upon us the charge of being fallen and depraved creatures, in need of deliverance from ruin. If this be so, surely our situation is most serious, demanding all that solemn consideration in regard to our acceptance with God, and our preparation for meeting him, which the holy Scriptures everywhere call upon us to exercise.

It has been your privilege, my dear sons, from your childhood, to be instructed in the way of salvation by Christ. But this is one of the great subjects in regard to which "line upon line, and precept upon precept," are found needful. You will not, therefore, I trust, consider it as superfluous to have your attention drawn to that great method of mercy, which the word of God styles "glad tidings of great joy to all people." And I hope, too, you will not forget that it is one thing to contemplate and acknowledge this method of mercy as a mere doctrinal statement, and quite another to receive it with gratitude and love, and make it the guide and joy of our lives.

The following statement may be considered as exhibiting that plan of acceptance with God, and of eternal life, with which you have been familiar from your youth up. O that it were impressed upon every heart connected with your institution, not merely as a system of theoretical belief, but as a plan of practical hope and life!

Man was made perfectly upright; in full possession of all the powers necessary to perfect moral agency, and with all the dispositions which prompted to a perfectly correct use of those powers. But "man being in honour abode not." He rebelled against God. He violated the covenant under which he was placed, and became liable to the dreadful penalty which it denounced against transgressors. In this fall of our first parents we are all sharers. Adam, as the covenant head of our race, bore a representative character. He was so constituted by a sovereign God; and when he fell, all his posterity fell with him. "In Adam," says the inspired apostle, "all die." "By one man's disobedience," he again declares, "many were made sinners." When our first father lost the holy image of God, he was of course incapable of transmitting it to us. We have, therefore, all totally lost our original righteousness; so that there is now, by nature, "none righteous, no not one." In short, we have all become guilty and polluted before God, and incapable of regaining his image or his favour by any merit or doings of our own. How, then, are we to be delivered from these deplorable circumstances? How shall we escape that wrath and curse which are the just penalty of sin? "How can we escape the damnation of hell?" In one word, how can those who must confess themselves to be sinners, miserable sinners, be saved? The law of God demands perfect obedience in thought, word, and deed, upon pain of death. It makes no allowance for the smallest delinquency or imperfection. Indeed, a Being of infinite purity cannot possibly demand less than perfection. To do this, would be to countenance sin. Nor can God set aside his own law, or permit his majesty and authority, as a righteous Governor, to be trampled under foot. To "clear the guilty," to take impenitent rebels, polluted with the love, as well as laden with the guilt of sin, into the arms of his love, would be to "deny himself." Where then is our refuge? Can God, consistently with his righteous character, forgive sin at all? If he can, how much, and under what circumstances, can he forgive? To these questions the light of nature can give no answer. Without the light of revelation, clouds and darkness rest upon all the conditions and prospects of our race.

But, blessed be God! "life and immortality are

brought to light through the gospel." Jehovah, in his infinite wisdom, power, and love, has devised and proclaimed a wonderful plan, by which sin was punished in our representative, while the sinner is pardoned; by which justice is completely satisfied, while mercy is extended to the guilty and vile; by which "grace reigns through righteousness unto eternal life, by Jesus Christ our Lord." This wonderful and glorious plan of mercy consisted in the Father giving his own Son to obey, suffer, and die in our stead, as our substitute; and in the Son consenting to take our place, to bear the penalty of the law in our stead, to "put away sin by the sacrifice of himself," and by his sufferings and obedience to purchase for us that justifying righteousness which we could never have wrought out for ourselves.

Such are the "glad tidings of great joy" which in the gospel are proclaimed to our fallen world; that the Lord Jesus Christ, the eternal Son of God, condescended, in his wonderful love, to assume our nature; to obey and suffer as our surety; to lift the penalty of sin from us, and take it on himself; and thus voluntarily to become the victim of divine justice in our stead. His language, in the eternal counsels of peace, was, "Let me suffer instead of the guilty; let me die to save them. Deliver them from going down to the pit; I will be their ransom." This wonderful, this unparalleled offer was accepted. The Father was well pleased for the righteousness' sake of his Son. He accepted his atoning sacrifice and perfect righteousness as the price of our justification; so that all who repent of sin, and believe in the name of this great Mediator, are "freely justified from all things, from which they could not be justified by the law of Moses"—that is by their own works of obedience. So that the Scripture may well say concerning the Saviour—"He is the end of the law for righteousness to every one that believeth. He is the Lord our righteousness. He was wounded for our transgression; he was bruised for our iniquities; the chastisement of our peace was upon him; and by his stripes we are healed. He bare our sins in his own body on the tree. He died the just for the unjust, that he might bring us to God. He delivered us from the curse of the law, being made a curse for us."

Here, then, my dear sons, is the only way of a sinner's return to God, and securing a title to eternal blessedness. In virtue of the covenant of redemption, the righteousness of Christ, or what he did and suffered on our behalf, is placed to the account of all who believe in him, as if they had performed it in their own persons. Though sinful and utterly unworthy in themselves, God is pleased to pardon and accept them as righteous in his sight, only for the righteousness' sake of his beloved Son. I am aware, indeed, that some who speak much of the "merits of Christ," and profess to rely entirely on those merits, represent the whole subject in a very different light. They suppose that, in consideration of the sufferings and death of our blessed Saviour, the original law of God, demanding perfect obedience, is repealed, and a mitigated law prescribed as the rule of our obedience. So that now, under the Christian dispensation, a perfect obedience is not required, but only an imperfect one, accommodated to our fallen nature and our many infirmities. But they insist that this imperfect obedience is the meritorious ground of our acceptance with God; and, of course, that eternal life is the purchase of our own works. In short, the doctrine of these errorists is, that the benefit conferred by the sufferings and death of Christ, consists, not in providing an entire righteousness for us, but only in abating the demands of the law; in bringing down the divine requirements more to a level with our ability, and still enabling us, low as we have fallen, to be the purchasers of salvation by our own obedience. Be assured this view of the subject is a grievous departure from the scriptural doctrine concerning the way of salvation. The Bible represents our pardon and acceptance with God as not founded, in any respect, or in any degree, on our own obedience; but as wholly of grace—as a mere unmerited gift, bestowed solely on account of what the Redeemer has done as our substitute and surety. It represents the holy law of God as remaining in all its original strictness, without repeal or mitigation; and as still falling with the whole weight of its penalty on all who have not taken refuge by faith in the Redeemer. But it declares the penalty to be removed from all who repent, and believe the gospel, not on account of any worthiness in themselves, as the meritorious ground of the benefit, but only on account of the perfect righteousness of Him who, "through the eternal Spirit, offered himself without spot to God." In short, the doctrine of the Bible is, that the holy character of God remaining unchangeably the same, and his law remaining without the least mitigation or abatement, the penitent and believing are accepted as righteous, solely on account of the obedience of the Mediator set to their account, and considered as wrought for them.

This righteousness of Jehovah the Saviour is said to be "to all, and upon all them that believe,"—that is, it is imputed to none, set to the account of none, but those who receive Christ by faith. Faith is that great master grace by which we become united to the Saviour, and his merits are made ours. This righteousness, therefore, is called "the righteousness of faith," and "the righteousness of God by faith." Hence we are said to be "justified by faith," and to be "saved by faith;" not that faith, as an act of ours, is in any measure the meritorious ground of our justification; but all these expressions imply that there is an inseparable connection, in the economy of grace, between believing in Christ, and being justified by him, or having his righteousness imputed to us. Happy, thrice happy they, who can thus call the Saviour theirs, and who have thus "received the atonement." From this hour, though unworthy in themselves, they are graciously pronounced righteous by their heavenly Judge, on account of what the Mediator has done. Their sins, though many, are for his sake forgiven them. They are "accepted in the Beloved." There is no condemnation to them now; and they shall find, to their eternal joy, that there is both safety and happiness in appearing clothed in the righteousness of Him who loved sinners, and gave himself for them, in "robes washed and made white in the blood of the Lamb."

But we not only need to be justified by the righteousness of Christ; we also indispensably need to be sanctified by the Spirit of Christ. We are by nature polluted as well as guilty. Accordingly the purification of our hearts, as well as the pardon of our sins, is one of the great benefits which the blessed Redeemer has purchased and secured by covenant to all believers. And for both these benefits the plan of mercy exhibited in the Gospel makes equal and effectual provision. "Whom he justifies them he also sanctifies." By the power of the Holy Spirit the dominion of sin is broken in the hearts of all who are brought under the power of the Gospel. The dominion of corruption in the soul is destroyed; the love of it is taken away; and though not perfectly sanctified in the present life, yet every believer has his sanctification begun. And it is carried on, not by his own wisdom or strength, but by the same divine power by which it was commenced; until he is, at last, made perfectly holy, as well as perfectly happy, in the presence of his God and Saviour.

Such, my dear sons, is that most interesting of all messages, which the religion of Jesus Christ brings to all who hear the Gospel. It charges us with being sinners—miserable sinners in the sight of God, without merit, without strength, and without hope in ourselves. It freely offers us peace, and pardon, and sanctification, and eternal life, "without money and without price," that is, as a free unmerited gift, "through the redemption that is in Christ Jesus." Its language is, "whosoever cometh to Him, he will in no wise cast out;"

and again, "whosoever will, let him come, and take of the water of life freely." It calls upon you to renounce all confidence in yourselves, and to receive and rest on Christ alone for salvation, as he is freely offered in the gospel. To this end, it is indispensable that you be convinced of sin; that you feel a deep and cordial sense of your own sinfulness and unworthiness; that you despair of saving yourselves; that you fall at the footstool of sovereign grace, feeling that you deserve to die, and that you can have no hope but in the atoning blood and sanctifying Spirit of the Redeemer. Until you are prepared to accept of Him with such convictions, and in this character; until you sincerely feel that you have nothing to plead but his merit, and humbly and gratefully rely on his grace and love for all that you need, you have yet to learn all that is practical and precious of this holy religion.

Say not, that our sinning and falling in Adam, and our recovery through the atoning sacrifice and righteousness of another, are mysteries which you cannot understand, and which are revolting to your minds. Surely it ought not to excite surprise or wonder in a reasonable being, that we should find mysteries in a plan of salvation contrived and made known by an infinite and incomprehensible God. But "let God be true, and every man a liar." What I have stated is plainly the doctrine of the word of God in relation to this great subject. It clearly informs us, that as in Adam we lost our innocence, and the divine favour, so through Christ, who is styled the "second Adam," we regain both the favour and image of God. "The mouth of the Lord hath spoken it." Let this suffice. Let us abhor the thought of being found "fighting against God."

But after all, do you ask, of what great value is this religion, that you should be urged with so much importunity to embrace it? I hope you will not be disposed to ask such a question; but if you should be, let me answer, its value is unspeakable, is infinite, for the present world, as well as the future; for "godliness is profitable unto all things, having the promise of the life that now is, as well as of that which is to come."

True religion is the only solid basis and pledge of good morals. I do not say, that there are no examples of unblemished morals among those who are not truly religious. Nor do I mean to assert, that all who claim to be religious are correct in their morals. But my meaning is, that the possession of true religion is the only sure pledge, the only effectual guaranty of sober deportment, of pure and exemplary morals, especially amidst the ardour and temptations of youth. It is a common maxim, among the men of the world, that "every man has his price." It cannot be denied, that, independently of the power of religion, there is too much reason for the adoption of this maxim. No one can be considered as safe from the allurements of sensuality, of avarice, or of ambition, unless fortified by principles drawn from the power and grace of God. There is absolutely no security, my dear sons, in anything short of this. We have all seen young men of the most elevated connections; of the finest talents; of the most excellent scholarship; of the very first general promise of character; and who seemed destined to adorn the highest stations;—we have seen them falling into habits of intemperance, gambling, fraud, lewdness, or some other degrading moral delinquency; gradually losing their reputation; losing their own self-respect; and either consigned by their vices to premature graves, or sunk, through the whole of their course, into wretchedness and infamy. When you think of such misguided and ruined youth, you may be ready to think, and to say, that you can rely on your own resolution to guard against such a ruinous course. But all confidence in anything, except religion, to preserve you from such courses, is fallacious and vain. And by religion here, I do not mean merely a profession of religion; for that will be no effectual safeguard to any one; we have seen professors, of more than ordinary apparent zeal, disgrace themselves and the name by which they were called. But I mean the possession of real practical religion—the religion of the heart. This is a real security. This will hold its possessor firmly and safely; and amidst all the storms of life, preserve from fatal shipwreck. We shall never hear of such a young man, that he has died a drunkard; or that he has been detected in base, mean, or swindling practices; or that he has become the companion of gamblers and blacklegs; or that he has murdered some acquaintance, or been murdered himself in a duel; or that he has been embarrassed and degraded by some licentious connection. No, we shall hear no such tidings of any such youth. He may not be rich; though he will be more likely to succeed in his temporal affairs than any other person. He may not be crowned with a large amount of worldly honour; though the probability is, that he will be more successful in this respect also, than the most of those who are destitute of religious principle. But he will be happy while he does live. He will be respected, and beloved, and useful. His latter end will be peace; and his name will be embalmed in the memory of the wise and the good, while the name of the wicked shall rot.

Further, true religion is the only adequate comforter under the sorrows and trials of life. These will come, in a greater or less degree, to all. The sanguine young man may, indeed, imagine, in the buoyancy of his hopes, that he shall never see sorrow; but that health, affluence, and pleasure shall mark his whole course. But if he "see many days, and rejoice in them all, let him remember the days of darkness, for they shall be many." There will be seasons of gloom and adversity to the most favoured. In those seasons where will be your refuge? Happy are those who, when the world frowns, when dangers threaten, when health gives way, when disappointments arise, can look up to a reconciled God and Father; can go to a throne of grace, and there leave every interest in the hands of infinite wisdom and goodness! It has been my happiness to see such young men; to see them adorning and enjoying the college to which you belong; and the recollection of the noble spirit and character which they presented, is now refreshing to the mind, especially when contrasted with the timidity, the weakness, and the comfortless character of the frivolous throng around them, in circumstances of similar trial. Montesquieu might well say, "How admirable is that religion which, while it seems only to have in view the felicity of another world, constitutes the happiness of the present!" Sir Humphry Davy, born in poverty, and in an obscure corner of England, was raised by industry and merit, unaided by friends, to such distinction, that he was chosen at the age of twenty-two, to fill the chair of chemistry in the "Royal Institution" of London. A few years afterwards he was elected President of the "Royal Society" of London, and stood confessedly at the head of the chemists of Europe. His testimony in favour of the consolations of religion is of the following decisive character: "I envy," says he, "no quality of the mind or intellect in others; not genius, power, wit, or fancy; but if I could choose what would be most delightful, and, I believe, most useful to me, I should prefer a firm religious belief to every other blessing; for it makes life a discipline of goodness;—creates new hopes when all earthly hopes vanish;—throws over the decay, the destruction of existence, the most precious of all lights;—awakens life even in death, and from corruption and decay calls up beauty and divinity;—makes an instrument of torture and shame the ladder of ascent to paradise;—and, far above all combinations of earthly hopes, calls up the most delightful visions of palms and amaranths, the gardens of the blessed, the security of everlasting joys, when the sensualist and the sceptic see only gloom, decay and annihilation." His last work—"Consolations in Travel," still more fully developes his highly interesting sentiments on this subject.

Finally; true religion is the only preparation and security for future and eternal blessedness. Can any thinking being, however young and buoyant in spirit, forget that he is soon to die, and bid farewell to all that he values here below? and that this event may take place before he has passed the age of adolescence? and that, of course, the interests of eternity are infinitely the most momentous? What is the body to the soul? What are all the transient joys of earth to the everlasting treasures of heaven? For those treasures and joys you can never be prepared, unless you have a taste and relish for them. Even if a holy God had not declared in his word, that "without holiness no man can see the Lord," the nature of the case would pronounce the same decision. No one can be happy but in his appropriate element. To imagine that any one can reach and enjoy a holy heaven, without some degree of meetness for the society and employments of that blessed world, is, of all delusions, one of the most preposterous and miserable. Our title to heaven is, as you have heard, what the Saviour has done and suffered for us as our surety. But our indispensable preparation for heaven, is that renewal of our nature by the Holy Spirit, which renders the presence and glory of God delightful to the soul. He who remains under the power of that carnal mind which is enmity against God, can be happy nowhere in the universe. Even if he could overleap the walls of the celestial paradise, it would be no heaven to him. He would still be constrained with anguish to say—
"Where'er I go is hell, myself am hell!"

These considerations, I have no doubt, will convince, have convinced, your judgment that religion is worthy of your supreme regard. Its claims are so obviously reasonable and powerful, that they can never be resisted by sober reasoning. But there is no delusion more common than that which tempts the young to postpone all attention to this subject to a future period. Knowing its importance, but "having no heart for it" at present, they are ready from day to day, to say to the serious monitor—"Go thy way for this time, when I have a more convenient season I will call for thee." Let me warn you against this procrastinating spirit, by which so many have been deceived and ruined. If religion be so precious as a guide, as a comforter, as a pledge of temporal prosperity and enjoyment, and as the indispensable means of eternal happiness—can you begin too soon to enjoy its benefits? If "the ways of wisdom are ways of pleasantness, and all her paths peace," is it wise to say, "Let me put off the attainment of this happiness to a future period?" Surely the sooner you begin to enjoy advantages so radical and precious, the better. Besides, have you any assurance that you will live to that age, or to see that concurrence of circumstances, which you fondly imagine will be more favorable to engaging in a life of piety than the present time? Not long since, a graduate of one of our colleges was heard to say—"I have finished my college education. I will now devote two years to the study of a profession; and then I will take one year to see what there is in that mighty thing they call *religion*." So calculated this blooming, sanguine youth. But before the time specified had half elapsed, he suddenly fell sick; was seized with delirium; and expired without hope. But why need I resort to the case of one with whom you had no personal acquaintance? Can you forget your own beloved brothers and sisters, removed in the morning of life; one of whom was cut down in a few weeks after his graduation, and when he was just entering on a course of professional study; and another at a still earlier stage of his education? What security have you that you will live to see another year? And even if you could be certain of living to old age, what reason have you to hope, if you go on neglecting religion, and hardening yourselves against its claims, that you will have grace given you, even in the decline of life, to "consider your ways?" O how many, who were in youth thoughtful and tender, have become more and more callous to every serious impression, as they advanced in life; and have at length sunk into the grave as destitute of hope as ever! Be entreated, then, my dear sons, now, while your hearts are comparatively tender; before the cares of the world have entwined around them a thousand entanglements; before you become hardened by inveterate habits of sin; be entreated to make choice of "that good part which can never be taken away from you."

I wish it were in my power, my beloved sons, to impart to you such views of this subject, as I am sure an enlightened attention to facts could not fail to give. Take up a college catalogue. O, it is a most instructive pamphlet! It affords a lively comment on all that I have told you about the uncertainty of life, and the folly of delaying to enter on the duties of true religion. Take it up, and look at the asterisk—that mournful mark of death, which stands opposite to the names of so many who received the honours of your college, within your own recollection. How some of them died, I am not able to tell you; but others departed, lamenting that they had not made more and earlier preparation for a dying hour, and that their time had been so much given to the vanities of the world. Will you not profit by such painful examples? "O that you were wise, that you understood these things, that you would consider your latter end!"

If you ask me, how that piety which is represented as so important, is to be attained, I answer, it is not the spontaneous growth of our nature. It is that to which we are naturally averse. It is the gift of God; and to be sought in the diligent use of those means which God has appointed for drawing near to him. The royal Psalmist asks—"Wherewith shall a young man cleanse his way?" And his answer is, "By taking heed thereto according to thy word." That is, it requires sincere and solemn application of mind to the subject, without which no one has a right to hope that he shall make the attainment.

The diligent perusal of the word of God is one of the most obvious and important of the means of grace. The Bible was given us to be a "light to our feet, and a lamp to our path." It exhibits, with unerring fidelity, every enemy, every snare, every danger which beset your path. It gives all the information, all the warning, all the caution, and all the encouragement which you need. It tells you, more perfectly than any other book, all that you have to fear, and all that you have to hope for. There is not a form of error or of corruption against which it does not put you on your guard; not an excellence or a duty which it does not direct you to cultivate and attain. No one ever made this holy book the guide of his life, without walking wisely, safely and happily; without finding the truest enjoyment in this world, and eternal blessedness in the world to come. But this is not all. The Bible is not only the word of life. It is not only that wonderful book which was sent from heaven to show us the way of salvation: it not only contains the glad tidings of pardon, and peace, and love, and glory to a lost world; and is, of course, worthy of the most grateful reception, and the most diligent and reverential study; but there is, besides, something in it which it becomes every aspirant to literary reputation duly to appreciate. It is full of the noblest specimens of literary beauty, and of tender, pathetic eloquence, that the world ever saw. There is something in it better adapted to touch the finest and best chords of human sensibility, to reach and sway the heart, than the most laboured products of rhetoric that the skill of man ever formed. I have known more than one case, in which secular orators have drawn from the figures and the language of the Bible their mightiest weapons, both for convincing the judgment, and captivating the hearts of their hearers; and am persuaded that he who does not study his

Bible, as well as his secular authorities, in preparing for public life, neglects a very important part of his education.

And in reading the Bible, I hope you will not forget that it is to be read with feelings, and in a manner very different from those with which you peruse all other books. If it be indeed inspired of God, and given to teach us the way of salvation, it surely ought to be read with serious and fixed attention; with unwearied diligence; with deep humility; with candid application to your own heart and conscience; and with devout application to the throne of grace, that you may be enabled to read it with understanding and with profit. Happy, thrice happy, is that youth who learns to go to the Bible for all his sentiments, principles, and rules of action; who searches its sacred pages daily for direction in his pursuits, for guidance in his perplexities, for comfort in his sorrows, and for help in every time of need. Such have the best pledge of temporal enjoyment, and of eternal blessedness.

Another important means by which you ought to seek the favour and image of God, is prayer. Need I dwell either on the duty or reasonableness of this exercise? If we are entirely dependent on God for every temporal and spiritual blessing, then it is surely reasonable that we should acknowledge our dependence, and apply to him with humility and earnestness for his aid. If his favour is life, and his blessings the best riches, it is evident that we ought to supplicate them with importunity and perseverance. If we are sinners, unworthy of the divine favour, we ought to humble ourselves at his footstool, and make confession of our sins with penitence, and a sincere desire to do better in time to come. If he has revealed a plan of mercy and grace to us, of which he invites and commands us to avail ourselves, then every principle of self-interest concurs with reason in urging us to seek with earnestness a participation in that mercy. And if our Maker and Redeemer has, in so many words, commanded us "by prayer and supplication with thanksgiving, to make known our requests to God," who can question, for a moment, the reasonableness of a compliance with that command?

I am afraid that many a youth who has been taught from his childhood to fear God, would be ashamed to be seen bowing his knees in secret before that Being whom his parents supremely love and venerate, and by whom he has been himself protected and sustained ever since he was born. Can it be necessary for me to demonstrate to you that this is a shame as foolish, as infatuated as it is criminal? Ashamed of acknowledging your Maker, your Sovereign, your constant Benefactor, who alone can make you happy, either in this world, or the world to come! O what insanity is here! It is to be ashamed of your true glory. A shame, the folly and infatuation of which can be equalled only by that which is manifested by the old as well as the young, viz., "glorying in their shame."

You will have no good reason to expect the blessing of God on your persons, your studies, or any of your interests, without feeling your need of that blessing, and importunately asking for it. Let no day, then, pass without at least two seasons of prayer. When you rise in the morning, implore the guidance and benediction of heaven on all the employments and privileges of the day; for you know not what may occur to disturb your peace, or endanger your character or improvement. And when you retire to rest at night, ask for the protection and blessing of Him who neither slumbereth nor sleepeth, over the repose of the night-watches. Nor are these the only proper objects of petition. Pray for your instructors; that they may be aided in their official work, and rewarded for all their labours of love. Pray for your fellow-students; that they may be imbued with a love of knowledge, with a love of order, and with all those fraternal and honourable dispositions which may render their society profitable and happy. Rely on it, the more you pray, the happier you will be. The more you make all around you the objects of your benevolent petitions, the more pleasant and profitable will be all your intercourse with them.

As another important means of grace, make a point of attending on the public worship of God, on every Lord's day, as well as on every other occasion when you have an opportunity so to do. Let no pretext for absenting yourselves from the house of God ever be admitted. On the one hand, those who habitually neglect it, manifest a spirit of disregard to the divine authority, which indicates a spirit most unpromising in regard to their spiritual interest. While, on the other hand, those who make conscience of being present with the people of God whenever they are assembled, manifest a reverence for his name and his worship, which we have reason to hope will issue in their happy preparation for his kingdom.

Let me further recommend that you be in the habit of statedly setting apart seasons of retirement, meditation, and self-examination in regard to your spiritual interests. I once heard of a young man who was remarkably thoughtless and dissipated, whose father in his last will bequeathed to him a large estate, on condition that he would, for so many years, spend half an hour every morning by himself, in serious reflection. The young man, in obedience to this injunction, began a compliance with it. At first it was a most unwelcome task, to which he forced himself as a means of holding his property. He soon submitted to it with less and less reluctance, until at length he adhered to it of choice, and became a truly virtuous and pious man.

The only other means of attaining the knowledge and love of God which I shall urge, is the reverential observance of the holy Sabbath. As the consecration of this day to rest from secular labours, and to the service of God, is one of the most important means of keeping the world in order, and maintaining the reign of religion among men; so the profanation of this day, is one of those sins which tend pre-eminently to banish religious sentiments from the mind, and to draw down the curse of heaven, both on individuals and society. There can be little hope, either of the success or the happiness of that individual, or that community, who habitually trample on that day which God has set apart for himself. The celebrated Lord Chief Justice Hale, equally distinguished as a jurist and a Christian, has left on record, "that he never prospered in any secular employment, unless it were a work of necessity or mercy, undertaken on the Sabbath; and, on the contrary, that the more closely he applied himself to the appropriate duties of that holy day, the more happy and successful were all the business and employments of the week following." The same, I am persuaded, will be the experience of every one who pays attention enough to this subject to mark the facts which occur in his own case. If, therefore, I were to hear that you were in the habit of pursuing your ordinary studies on the Sabbath, or of engaging in the secular amusements in which many profanely indulge on that day, I should expect to hear little good, either of your moral or religious character, and should have little hope of your ultimate success, even in your intellectual pursuits. Rely upon it, you will never gain by robbing God, or by profaning any of his institutions.

My dear sons, consider these things. The blessing of God is the best riches, and he addeth no sorrow with it. That blessing can never be expected, unless you sincerely seek and attain true religion. "It is, therefore, not a vain thing for you; it is your life." Upon this hangs everything precious, everything truly valuable for both worlds. There have, indeed, been instances of men, who had no religion, enjoying much temporal aggrandizement, and no small degree of honour among men. But how much happier would they have been, and how much more solid honour and confidence might they have enjoyed, had they been sincere Christians, living habitually under the influence, and enjoying the consolations, of the gospel of Christ! Sir Walter Scott, and even the cold-blooded infidel, Byron, each attained a distinction in his day, which many a youth has been tempted to envy. But was either of them a happy man? Especially was not the author of "Childe Harold" regarded by every sober-minded contemporary, as, with all his talents, no better than a fiend incarnate? And when we come to the death-bed of both, what do we see but the absence of that hope and comfort which every wise man desires to enjoy in his last hour?

My dearly beloved sons! You must one day be serious, whether you will or not. At present the vanities of the world may absorb your attention, and hide more important objects from your view. But, be assured, the time is approaching when you will see things in a very different light. The fashion of this world is rapidly passing away. Scenes untried and awful are about to open before you. Death, judgment and eternity are hastening on apace. Then, when the sources of earthly comfort are dried up; when heart and flesh begin to fail; when you are about to bid an everlasting farewell to this world, and all its vanities; then, if not before, you will certainly lament the want of sober consideration. Then, if not before, you will cry out in the bitterness of remorse, "O that I had been wise, that I had thought of this, that I had considered my latter end!" Here, then, I must leave you, "commending you to God, and to the word of his grace, which is able to enlighten your mind; to give you an heart to serve him; and to prepare you for an inheritance amongst all them that are sanctified."

LETTER VI.

REBELLIONS.

Ars cujus principium est mentiri, medium laborare, finis poenitere. ANON.

———Facilis descensus Averni;
Sed revocare gradum,———
Hoc opus, hic labor est. ÆNEID, VI. 126.

MY DEAR SONS—Though you have never been witnesses of one of those grand rebellions, of which the history of our college has furnished some examples, yet you have seen enough of the elements and the inceptive workings of such insanity, to form a tolerable estimate of its real character. And I think I may venture to say, that the more you have seen of the causes and spirit of such lawless outbreakings, the less you have respected them, and the more you have been disposed to contemplate their fomentors and their conductors with mingled feelings of contempt and abhorrence. And I can assure you, my dear sons, if it were possible to impart to you the more intimate knowledge that I have had of the commencement, the history, and the termination of all such scenes as have occurred in the college with which you are connected, within the last forty years, your impressions of their folly and wickedness would be still deeper and more abhorrent.

Few things are more adapted to show both the infatuation and the atrocity of rebellions in college, than recurring to the origin of most of them. A great majority of them arise from a desire on the part of students, otherwise orderly, to shield from merited discipline the corrupt and profligate of their fellows. A few, perhaps, of the unprincipled and habitually disorderly students have justly incurred the infliction of severe discipline—suspension, or expulsion from the institution. The delinquents have, it may be, some talents, much impudence; and that desperate recklessness which makes them anxious, if they must go, to have companions both in crime and in suffering. A number of their fellow students, perhaps a large number, are fools enough to be made the dupes of these profligates; to make a common cause with them, and to resolve to share their fate. The consequence is, that they do share their fate. All that belong to the combination are sent away from college; and are so far from gaining the end for which they combined, that the result is permanent and hopeless disgrace. Such is the usual history, and such the invariable result of college rebellions. In a few instances, the loss of life, either to some of the rebels, or of the faculty, has been the deplorable consequence.

Now, in this whole matter, there is an amount of complicated folly and wickedness, which it is not easy to measure. For, in the first place, as to the original offenders, in whose behalf all this mischief has been perpetrated, they are commonly profligate villains, who ought not to belong to any decent institution, and whose defence, in any form, is infamy; villains who, instead of being undeservedly or too hastily visited with discipline, ought, perhaps, long before to have been sent off in disgrace. In the second place, every step taken by this combination, is a high-handed and peculiarly criminal opposition, not only to the laws which its members are bound to obey, but to a faculty, as it were, in mass, who are labouring day and night to promote their welfare, and who are individually and collectively distressed by the insubordination. And in the third place, it is an act of wanton and voluntary suicide. Those who combine and make a common cause with the original delinquents, plunge into the gulf, for the sake of those who have neither generosity nor honesty enough to thank them for the sacrifice, and thus, perhaps, destroy all their own prospects for life, besides inflicting a wound on the hearts of parents or guardians which can never be healed on this side of the grave.

Nor is this all. No one can tell, when he connects himself with a scene of this kind, but that it may terminate, as was before intimated, in the loss of life. Many months have not elapsed, since, in a rebellion which took place in the university of a neighbouring state, a beloved and highly valued professor lost his life by the murderous hand of a profligate student; and how often the most valuable lives have been put in imminent danger in similar scenes of insubordination and violence, he who is even tolerably acquainted with their history, well knows. How infatuated, then, as well as criminal, must be that youth who allows himself to engage in a plan of resistance to lawful authority, which he cannot but know may terminate in the destruction of his own life, or in that of one or more other individuals, a thousand times more precious to their friends and to the community than his own!

The following statement, perfectly in point, cannot fail of commanding the most respectful consideration from every reader who knows the high character of the writer, and who recollects that he speaks on this subject from the most ample experience. The venerable writer speaking of himself, says:—

"At the age of seventeen he left, for the first time, the house of the best of mothers, to go to Princeton College; and with the sincerest resolution to fulfil all her anxious wishes in his behalf. Towards the close of the first session, some very unworthy young men were dismissed. They contrived, however, to impose upon the great body of the others, and to induce them to believe that they were most unjustly and cruelly treated. What was called a petition was gotten up in their behalf, and offered for the signatures of the rest.

Great numbers signed it, scarce knowing its contents. It proved to be such a one as the faculty could not with propriety listen to, or allow to pass unnoticed. We were required to withdraw our signatures; and it was so managed by the leaders of the rebellion, that the college was broken up in confusion, and all returned home. It was then that I felt the excellence of maternal authority, which great numbers felt not, for they did not return. My excellent mother, though mild, yet firm, as she was wont to be, bade me go back, and make atonement for the evil committed. And I went, and confessed my fault, and still live to exhort other parents, and other sons to 'go and do likewise.' As a warning to the young men of our land, let me say, that it required nearly thirty years to repair the injury done to that institution, by that proceeding of unreflecting and misguided youths. Let me warn them to beware how they ever assemble together for the purpose of consulting how to redress the supposed wrongs of their fellow-students; and, above all, how they set their names to any instrument purporting to be a condemnation of those in authority. Very seldom, indeed, will the faculty mistake in their judgments concerning those who are the subjects of discipline. All of those for whom the petition alluded to was offered, proved to be most unworthy characters; and in my many and extensive journeys throughout the length and breadth of our land, since that time, I have met with very many of those who were most zealous in the cause, but never with one who did not condemn and regret the part which he had taken in it."*

Such is the faithful testimony of an eye and ear witness, nay of a deep temporary partaker in the evil deplored. I also, though never, at any period of my college course, a participant in such a scene, can bear

* "Religious Education," a tract by the Right Rev. William Meade, Bishop of the Protestant Episcopal Church in the diocese of Virginia.

testimony equally explicit and to the same amount. My observation, in all cases, goes to establish the following points:

1. I have never known the rebels to carry their point; that is, I have never known an instance in which they gained the object for which they combined. One of the laws of our college is in the following words:

"If any clubs or combinations of the students shall at any time take place, either for resisting the authority of the college, interfering in its government, or for executing or concealing any evil or disorderly design, every student concerned in such combination, shall be considered as guilty of the offence which was intended; and the faculty are empowered and directed to break up all such combinations as soon as discovered, and to inflict a severer punishment on each individual than if the offence intended had been committed in his individual capacity, whatever may be the number concerned, or whatever may be the consequence to the college."

This law, as far as my knowledge extends, has been uniformly acted upon in our college. In two instances, within my recollection, it became necessary to disband the entire body of the students. But the rebels always went home without attaining their object.

2. In almost all cases—indeed I remember no real exception—the leading rebels turned out not only unworthy, but profligate, degraded and miserable. The proud contrivers and chief conductors of insurrection against college authority, may glut their diabolical vengeance; may give much trouble to those whom they dislike; may destroy much property; nay, may destroy life. But one thing is certain—their own infamy is hopelessly sealed. Their career generally shows that the frowns of man, and the curse of God rest upon them without remedy. If I could but give you the simple unvarnished history of a few of these mock heroes, after the catastrophe which led to their expulsion from college, it would stand in the place of a

thousand arguments against all such wicked and insane projects.

3. I can also verify the statement of Bishop Meade, that I have never known any student who had the remotest connection with any rebellious combination, who did not afterwards deeply regret his conduct, and condemn himself for it without reserve.

4. Had you been trustees of our college as long as I have been, (now between thirty and forty years,) you would have been witnesses of some of the most painful conflicts, connected with this subject, which can well be encountered by men who have a paternal feeling for the welfare of youth. Young men who had suffered themselves to partake in the unlawful and disorganizing combinations which have been described, and had been subjected to the sentence of expulsion from the college, have returned, after the lapse of twenty years and more, and earnestly requested—not indeed to be received again as students—but to have the sentence of expulsion revoked, and the painful record of their disgrace borne by the college records obliterated. You may well suppose that a board made up of serious benevolent men, ready to take every obstacle which they conscientiously could out of the way of a returning penitent, would feel no little pain in denying such a request from one who appeared to come with a proper spirit, and who had done all he could to atone for his crime by the sober and exemplary living of many years. But it was impossible to comply with such a request. As well might a man who had been convicted of theft or forgery, by a court of justice, twenty years ago, but had ever since, after suffering the penalty of the law, manifested a penitent and blameless life—come and ask the court to revoke its sentence, and expunge its record of his crime and conviction. The reply of Chief Justice Hale, when importuned to have mercy on a weeping culprit, was a just and noble one—"While I wish to show mercy to him, I feel bound also to have mercy

on my country." What would become of a college which should consent thus to reverse her sentences, and whitewash the traitors who had striven to destroy her? Her authority would soon be despised, and her discipline a nullity. "The way of transgressors is indeed hard," and one of the many proofs of this is, that from the bitter consequences of many sins the culprits can never escape. The grave may hide their bodies from view; but the memory of their crimes and their shame will be as imperishable as the records of justice can make them.

You are now, I trust, my dear sons, after pondering on what has been said on this subject, in some measure prepared to receive and profit by the paternal counsels which naturally flow from the foregoing considerations. They are these:

1. Always take for granted that the faculty are right in their requisition and in their discipline. They are commonly better informed than any one of the students, perhaps than all of them put together. They are far better judges than the students can be, as to what is safe and proper, and tends to the real good of the institution. They are far more impartial than the subjects of discipline are likely to be. And they are incomparably more attached to the interests of the college, than you or any other student. It will, therefore, be, on every account, safest and wisest always to take for granted, as a matter of course, that they are right; and that you have nothing to do but to obey. The exceptions to this fixed principle will ever be found so "few and far between," that it may be safely assumed as a maxim that will seldom fail.

2. Never listen to the complaints or the accusations of such of your fellow students as have been visited with the lash of discipline. You may rest assured that nothing of this kind comes upon any young man without a cause. Turn away from his story. Encourage him not. Allow him not for one moment to imagine that he has gained either your confidence or your approbation.

3. Never attend any meeting of students called to petition for a redress of grievances at the hand of the faculty, unless it be, with dignified independence, to remonstrate in toto, and on principle, against the measure. A redress of grievances, if such really exist, will be much more likely to be obtained by the private application of a few orderly students, than by a public and noisy combination. Put your name to no paper creating or encouraging any such combination. It may appear harmless and even commendable at first, but you know not to what it may grow. "The beginning of evil is like the letting out of water." That which appeared in the commencement a small and perfectly manageable rill, may soon become an overwhelming torrent, and bear away all before it.

4. Never let it be borne to future times by the records of Nassau Hall, that a son of your parents had affixed to his name, and to theirs, the stigma, that he had risen in rebellion against his *Alma Mater*, and had suffered the only capital punishment which a treason so base could incur—expulsion.

There are, no doubt, other sources and forms of rebellion than those which have been specified; but they may all be reduced to the same general principles, and may all with propriety be treated in the same general manner. Sometimes they originate in dissatisfaction with the diet in the public refectory; sometimes from the extent of the lessons assigned to the several classes; and again, at other times, from the refusal of some solicited privilege or indulgence. Now it would be wrong to assert that the faculty of any college is infallible, or that either their interdicts or their prescriptions are always, of course, to be considered as right. But the fact is, that, even if, from error in judgment, they should sometimes happen to be wrong, it is a much smaller evil, in practice, to assume that in any given case they are right, and to decide and act accordingly, than to allow the students to sit in judgment upon their decisions and doings, and thus to be judges and jurymen in their own cause. The most learned and conscientious jurists presiding in a civil court, may decide erroneously. But suppose they do, what is the appropriate remedy? To raise a mob in the court-house? to explode gunpowder among the multitude, at the risk of life? and to destroy the chairs, tables, and other furniture of the building? Would any of these either rectify the error in question, or promote the cause of substantial justice? The very suggestion of such a method of redress is at once contemptible and shocking; and those who should resort to it, would be deemed a set of silly infatuated savages. If the decision complained of is to be reversed, the reversal is to be obtained by other and more peaceable measures. All the violence tends but to mischief, and must be severely punished, or there will be an end of order and of justice.

Precisely such are the principles which ought to be laid down concerning the decisions of a college faculty. They are probably right; but, whether right or wrong, the very worst judges in the case are the rash, inexperienced, and headstrong subjects of discipline. If every wayward child is permitted to review and reverse the sentences of wise and faithful parents, it is plain that domestic government and order will soon cease, and all parties be less safe and less happy. If unwise or oppressive measures on the part of the immediate government of a college are supposed by the reflecting and orderly portion of the pupils to exist, the only measures which ought to be thought of are two; one, to send a small and respectful committee, made up of two or three of the students known to be among the most respected and confided in by the faculty, to present the humble statement and request of the whole body; and if this be not successful, the second step should be to appeal to the board of trustees. If by neither of these methods the object of the complainants can be obtained, the presumption is, either that the evils complained of are imaginary, or that, for the time being, they do not admit of a remedy. I have no recollection of any case in which an appeal to the board of trustees was followed with success to the appellants. The truth is, the faculty of every college are always under the temptation to go as far as they possibly can, consistently with duty, to gratify the students. Their own popularity and ease will, of course, in ordinary cases, induce to this. Seldom indeed will a calm and impartial body of guardians, having nothing to do with immediate instruction, lean more than they to the side of indulgence.

There is a species of conduct on the part of students which sometimes occurs, which may, perhaps, be as appropriately mentioned in this letter as in any other. I refer to the case of those students who, in their own estimation, and in that of their friends, are considered as having high claims to distinguished rank in the assignment of college honours: and when honours adequate to their expectations are not awarded to them, undertake to resent it as gross injustice, and either attempt to excite a mutiny in their behalf, or decline to receive the honour assigned them, and perhaps even refuse to speak at all at the ensuing commencement, and forfeit their graduation altogether. There is in all this an arrogance and presumption unworthy of young gentlemen approaching the age of manhood. Who are the best judges of a student's proper merits and rank—himself, or the faculty, who have been watching over him, and labouring with him for years? It is very possible, indeed, that a faculty may be guilty of great injustice in this matter. From some cause, and perhaps not a very laudable one, they may award to a candidate for graduation a rank decisively below that to which he is fairly entitled. But what then? Is he or the faculty the regularly constituted judge in the case? Every one knows it is the faculty. Will he be likely, then, to gain anything by resenting their award, or refusing to submit to it? I will not venture to pronounce that no degree of injustice can warrant a student in refusing to submit to it. But I have no recollection of having ever known such a case. Amidst all the instances of insubordinate conduct on such occasions which have come to my knowledge, I have never known one case in which the student who adopted this course gained any advantage by it. They have, in every case, lost the object which they sought, and been regarded by all their enlightened and impartial friends as acting an unwise part.

LETTER VII.

HEALTH.

"Non est vivere, sed valere vita.

My Dear Sons—I need not say a word to you of the value of health. All know it. All acknowledge it. If I were to attempt formally to prove it, you would consider me as undertaking a needless task. And yet a large portion of mankind, and especially of the young, appear to be so unmindful of the value of this blessing, and so reckless of its preservation, that there is hardly any subject in regard to which unceasing lessons are more needed, or are given from time to time with less benefit.

I once felt inclined to enter into cautions and counsels on this subject very much in detail; but a growing impression of the difficulty of doing justice to it, and a fear of doing mischief by multiplying advices respecting it, induce me to be much more brief than I originally intended. All that I shall attempt is to give a few brief hints, which I hope will not be in vain; but which, at the same time, I fear you will not appreciate as you ought, until the unhappy consequences of rejecting them shall practically impress them on your minds.

There are two extremes on this subject, to which young men are prone; against both I am earnestly desirous of guarding you. The one is to imagine that the citadel of their health is impregnable; that no care of it is necessary; that they may take any liberties with it, and lay any burdens upon it that they please. This mistake leads to unlimited exposure, and an utter disregard of all care and caution in avoiding the sources of disease. Hence it has happened that some of the most Herculean young men I have ever known, have been among the most short-lived; simply because they had so much confidence in their health and strength, and were so persuaded that they could bear anything, that they took no care of themselves, until the finest constitutions were wrecked and destroyed. Some of the most striking examples of this have occurred, not only in Nassau Hall, but also in the classes with which you are familiar; examples to which I cannot refer without the most mournful recollections.

The other extreme to which I alluded, is that of those who imagine that great scrupulousness of attention, and the most vigilant care of health, are necessary to its preservation; that a multitude of rigid cautions, a frequent resort to medicine, guarding against all exposure to cold and damp weather; close and warm rooms, much wrapping up, &c. &c., are indispensable. The young man who acts upon this plan, will probably soon render himself a miserable invalid for life, if he do not speedily cut short his days. The truth is, that in this, as in a thousand other things, we may err as much, and as fatally, in over-doing as in under-doing; and the path of wisdom is that of a happy medium between extremes.

There are some general principles in the preservation of health, to which I am earnestly desirous of directing your attention, and which, when they are regarded with enlightened and discriminating care, may be considered as comprehending all others. Of these general principles, I shall now trouble you with only four, viz:—Be strictly temperate with regard to aliment. Take, every day, a large amount of gentle exercise. Carefully guard against all intestinal constipation. And always avoid too much warmth, both in your clothing and your apartment, quite as vigilantly as you do too much exposure to cold.

1. With regard to the first, remember that temper-

ate eating in you, is a very different thing from what it is in a day-labourer. The latter may, in common, safely and even profitably, take two or three times the amount of aliment, that can be ventured upon by a student, or by any sedentary person. If a given portion of solid food be found to oppress you, gradually diminish the quantity, carefully watching the effect, until you ascertain the quantity which is best suited to your constitution, and after taking which you feel most vigorous, active and comfortable, both in body and mind. It is plain that this matter can be regulated only by the individual himself; and that it requires daily watchfulness and resolution. Many students, I have no doubt, injure their health, and some bring themselves, I am persuaded, to premature graves, by over-eating, as really as others do by over-drinking. The effects of the former species of excess are not quite so manifest, or quite so disreputable as those of the latter; but, in a multitude of cases, they are no less fatal. And especially ought this strict guard, as to the quantity and quality of the aliment taken, to be exercised by those who cannot be persuaded to take the requisite amount of bodily exercise. To eat without restraint, while the latter is neglected, is perfect madness. The answer of Sir Charles Scarborough, physician to Charles II., to one of the courtiers of that monarch, is worthy of being remembered—"You must eat less, or take more exercise, or take physic, or be sick." This enlightened man, physician to a profligate king, and a no less profligate court, presented the only alternatives by which the safety of our bodily condition can be secured. If I had a thousand voices, I would proclaim this response in every college, and to every studious young man in the land. However little it may be regarded, the diet of a student is of more importance than can easily be described. It ought always to be simple. Luxuries, and especially a multiplicity of artificial dishes, and the refinements of confectionery, ought to be avoided with sacred care. Dr. Franklin always lived on the simplest food, and with the strictest guard against every inordinate indulgence. We are also told that his habit was to go without his dinner one day in every week. This he called "giving nature a holiday;" that his stomach might not be injured by being kept too constantly at hard work.

If at any time you feel unwell, stop eating until you are better. This was the practice of Bacon, of Napoleon, and of a host of other eminent men, with whose histories we are familiar. When they were attacked with feverish feelings, they either fasted strictly, for twenty-four or even forty-eight hours; or at any rate, took nothing but a few spoonfuls of some simple liquid to sustain nature, and to allay the importunity of hunger, until their morbid sensations were removed. Few people are aware that, when they are sick, food does them little or no good, or rather only adds to the burden of the febrile affection. I have no doubt that a large portion of diseases, and especially of those which attack the youthful frame, where there is no morbid diathesis of a chronic character, would readily yield to a day or two of rigid fasting alone. It is because few people can endure the self-denial requisite for this purpose, that they prefer the removal of their ailments by the extemporaneous application of the lancet, or the stores of the *materia medica*. This is a very impolitic plan of procedure. It is violently interfering with the regular order of our frame, when the *vis medicatrix naturæ*, if left to itself, would do the work much better. These remarks are of course not intended to apply to cases of violent attacks of inflammatory disease, where congestion, or lesion in vital organs, indicated by much pain, is to be apprehended; but chiefly to those cases in which obscure feverish feelings indicate the approach, rather than the decisive onset of disease. In cases which mark the approach, or the actual attack of acute disease, medical advice ought to be sought without loss of time.

2. The importance of taking a large portion of gentle exercise every day, can scarcely be overrated.

Every student who wishes to preserve good health and spirits, ought to be moving about in the open air from three to four hours daily. You may live with less, and, possibly, enjoy tolerable health. But if you wish fully to possess the *mens sana in corpore sano*, of which the Latin poet speaks, rely upon it, with most students, less will not answer. I have said that your exercise ought to be gentle. Some students, after exhausting themselves by a protracted period of severe study of some hours, start from their seats, issue forth, and engage in some violent exercise, which throws them into a profuse perspiration, from which they can scarcely escape with impunity. In many such cases, they had much better have continued to sit still. After coming to a pause in my exertion, and resuming my seat, I have found it difficult to avoid taking cold, unless I would continue the perspiration, or the state of temperature approaching it, by wrapping myself up in a cloak, and remaining so until the perspiration had entirely subsided. This is a precaution which is troublesome, and will be submitted to by few.

Your exercise ought to bear strict proportion to your constitution and your habits. Gentle exercise, diffused through three or four hours, is much better adapted to a sedentary man, than a concentration of the same amount of muscular motion, within a single hour or less. It is also worthy of remark, that exercise taken either immediately before, or immediately after eating, is both less comfortable, and less valuable, than if at least an hour of rest be suffered to intervene. No prudent traveller will feed his horse immediately after his arrival at the place of baiting; or, if he can avoid it, put him on the road again as soon as he has swallowed his food. The same principle applies to all animal nature.

But there is a class of cases, in regard to exercise, to which a special reference ought to be made here. Sometimes young men come to college, who have been accustomed to active, and, it may be, to laborious lives in the pure air of the country, and who commence study with firm and florid health. Scarcely any, in this situation, are fully aware of the danger they encounter in sitting down to close intellectual application. I have often known a constitution the most robust, suddenly to give way, in six or nine months after this change of habit, and become utterly broken and prostrated. The truth is, a young man of the most robust and florid health, who addresses himself suddenly to a season of close study, is more apt—contrary to the common impression—far more apt to suffer severely from close mental and sedentary occupation, than one of a more lax fibre, and long accustomed to study. I can call to mind some of the most melancholy examples of this fact, in which, from not being apprised of the principle which it involves, the calamity came on almost with the suddenness and violence of a whirlwind, before the sufferers were aware.

3. My third advice has a respect to intestinal constipation. There can be no health, where this is suffered long to continue. And yet it is a point to which few inexperienced students are as attentive as they ought to be. They either neglect it, until a decisive indisposition convinces them of their folly; or they are very frequently endeavouring to remove it by the use of medicine. Both methods of treating the difficulty are miserably ill-judged. Medicine ought to be the last resort; and is seldom necessary, unless where there has been great mismanagement. Gentle exercise, abstemiousness, and the judicious use of mild dietetical aperients, (which are different with different people, and must be matter of experiment,) form the system which a little experience will show you to be the best. If, instead of this course, you go on eating as usual, and adhere as closely to your seat as at other times, you will probably not escape a serious indisposition.

4. The temperature of your room, and of your body,

is the last of the general principles in reference to health, to which I shall request your attention. A student, whose robustness is almost always in some degree impaired by sedentary habits, ought never to allow himself, if he can avoid it, to sit in a cold room, or in a current of cold air. I think I have known some young persons to contract fatal diseases by inadvertently allowing themselves to occupy such a situation even for a short time, especially when heated. But it is nearly, if not quite, as unfriendly to health, for a student to allow himself to be overheated, either by the atmosphere of a room excessively warmed, or by too great a load of clothing, either in bed or out of it. Everything of this kind ought to be carefully avoided. So far as my own experience goes, I am constrained to say, that excessive heat has been quite as often to me the source of disease, as excessive cold. He who is about to take a long walk, in the course of which he has an opportunity of keeping himself warm by constant, vigorous motion, ought just as carefully to avoid covering himself with an overcoat while his walk continues, as he ought to be to avoid sitting in a cold place, or in a draft of air, at the end of his walk, without it. No ceremony, no consideration whatever, ought to prevent his avoiding such a place, in such circumstances, with the most scrupulous decision.

You will gather from the foregoing remarks, that my plan for preserving health, is by no means that of tampering with medicines, or of perpetual nursing, or wrapping up, and avoiding the open air; a plan much more likely to make a valetudinarian, than a man of good health; but that of employing wisely and vigilantly the great art of prevention. Those who are already favoured with good health, and a sound constitution, ought to study to retain the blessings, by avoiding every species of excess, and by guarding against every approach to a derangement of the system; and, under the blessing of God, all will be well.

But while I give these counsels in regard to the

general health, I feel that there is no less need of some advices concerning particular organs of the body, which are exceedingly apt to suffer from the want of skill or attention in their management.

There is no organ of the human body more apt to become disordered by indiscreet or careless use than the eyes. What with protracted night studies, the unskilful use of candle and lamp-light, the reading of much small and indistinct print, and the prolonged and overstrained application of the eyes in any way, they are so much injured by many students before they leave college, that they are, in a great measure, disabled from the enjoyment of study for the remainder of their lives. It is well known that the justly celebrated President Dwight, by the excessive use of his eyes by candle-light, while he was in college, brought on a disease of that organ from which he never recovered, which gave him much pain, and compelled him to employ the eyes of others in a large part of the studies of his subsequent life.

In regard to this subject I would earnestly recommend to your attention the following counsels.

Avoid as much as you possibly can studying by candle-light. Begin your studies with the dawn of day, and improve every moment of day-light that you can secure. Study at a late hour at night ought never to be indulged in by any one who values his health. Two hours' sleep before midnight are worth three if not four after it. He who allows himself frequently to remain at his studies after ten o'clock in the evening, is probably laying up in store for himself bitter repentance.

Further, beware, in night studies, of the use of such lamps, or other lights, as, by means of reflectors, pour an intense light on your book or paper. Lamps or other lights of this kind, furnished with shades, while they undoubtedly shield the eyes from injury, by the direct rays of light, which is the object aimed at, are apt to do much more injury, by rendering the reflected light more vivid and dazzling. In fact, instead of protecting or favouring the eyes, they are apt to impair the soundest vision, and have proved in many cases extremely hurtful. If a shade be used at all, it ought not to be placed on the lamp or candlestick itself, for the purpose of casting the light down with more intensity; but on the forehead of the student, merely to prevent the direct rays of light from striking on his eyes. Indeed, a common hat itself would be one of the best screens with which to read or write at night, were it not for the danger of keeping the head too warm, and thus laying the foundation of various countervailing evils. This is mentioned only for the purpose of pointedly warning against it. A very light shade, made to fasten over the eyes, without covering the head, would be in every respect preferable.

Let me advise you to do all your writing in a standing posture. This has been my own constant practice for nearly fifty years; and I am constrained, from ample experience, to recommend it as attended with many advantages. If you write at a common table, the probability, and certainly the danger is, that you will contract a crooked, half-bent mode of sitting, which will materially injure your health. Writing-chairs are very much in vogue with many students. But, if I am not greatly deceived, they are pestiferous things, which do ten times as much harm as good. It is almost impossible to write on them without incurring an unequal and mischievous pressure on one side. Indeed, a gentleman of much experience and careful observation lately assured me, that he had procured almost the entire banishment of such chairs from an important literary institution, with which he was connected, on account of the serious mischief which he found them to produce to the persons and general health of the student. If you write standing, and guard against pressing the breast bone on the edge of the desk, but rest altogether on your arms, I am persuaded you will find it a method attended with fewer inconveniences and dangers than any other. On this plan, no part of the body is in a constrained posture, and the circulation is wholly unobstructed. Besides, if you read sitting, as most people do, it will create an agreeable variety if you rise when you begin to write.

Pay particular attention to your teeth. By this I do not mean that you should be continually going to the dentist; and far less that you should abound in applications to the teeth of various tooth-powders, which too commonly partake of acid qualities, which cannot fail of corroding, and of course injuring them. I believe that, in most cases, applying a little clean water, in which a small portion of common salt has been dissolved, with a soft brush, to the teeth, on rising in the morning, and just before retiring to rest at night, will be quite sufficient to preserve a pure and healthful state of the mouth. The evils arising from the neglect or mismanagement of the teeth are not only numerous, but most serious. Diseased gums and teeth, fetid breath, toothache, early loss of teeth, interfering with the mastication of food, and destroying the power of distinct articulate speech, are among the natural and inevitable results. Often, very often, have I seen fine young men, who had originally strong and beautiful sets of teeth, from gross negligence, or from unhappy management, presenting diseased and offensive mouths before they were twenty-five, and obliged to come forward, to the pulpit or the bar, with mouths full of substitutes provided by the dentist, which, though exceedingly valuable, are both defective and troublesome.

In my letter on temperance, I have dwelt largely on the importance of that virtue to health, and earnestly hope that my sons will seriously regard my counsels on this subject, for the sake of their physical, as well as their moral welfare. But there are various stimulants beside strong drink, against which I would put you on your guard. The moderate use of common salt is, I believe, generally considered by wise physiologists as indispensable to the healthful condition of animal life;

and it therefore ought to enter, under proper regulation, into our daily food. But this regulation is exceedingly important. The excessive use of this article has led to serious evils, and must be considered as highly insalubrious. I dislike to see young persons using mustard, pepper, and especially cayenne pepper, as necessary to give their food an acceptable relish. All these things, together with the pungent oriental soys, and pickles, I would advise you never to use; or at any rate never to use them habitually or freely. They are all stimulants, and some of them highly stimulating in their character; and of course their tendency is largely to expend the sensorial power of the human system, and prematurely to wear out the vital principle. Perhaps it may be said that some very pleasant dishes require condiments of this kind, to assist digestion and render them safely eatable. But surely every wise student, if he values his constitution, and desires to enjoy comfortable health, will rather abstain from dishes which require a very vigorous stomach to digest, than resort to violent and injurious means for rendering them harmless.

The ways in which young men in college endanger their health are so numerous, that it is difficult to go sufficiently into detail to meet all cases. But there is one habit so replete with danger, and yet so common, that I feel constrained to single it out for warning,—I mean the practice of sitting, and especially lying on the damp ground, in warm weather;—a practice from which severe diseases, and the loss of life have often been derived. It is indeed wonderful that thinking youth are so often found indulging in this perilous imprudence.

Lying long in bed in the morning, is very unfriendly to health and long life. It is at once a symptom and a cause of feeble digestion, of nervous debility, and of general languor. Whereas, early rising is commonly connected with sound sleep, with elasticity of body and mind, and with habits of activity, which are greatly conducive both to health and comfort. Nor is this practice less conducive to success in mental improvement. It not only tends to give a daily spring to the mind, but also to make a very important addition to the studying hours of the student, and to promote long life. It was the remark, if I mistake not, of the celebrated Lord Mansfield, that illustrious English judge, that among all the very aged men whom he had been called to examine in his court, he could not recollect one that was not an early riser.

I have only one advice more to offer in regard to your health. It is that you never pursue your studies to the length of exhaustion; that you never urge yourselves to the fulfilment of a prescribed task when sickness renders all mental effort painful and oppressive. By such pressure the mind is jaded and injured, and no valuable acquisition can be made. It is not only up-hill work; but any real progress, in these circumstances, is seldom made. In all mental efforts it is best to leave off before reaching the point of fatigue. When we go on beyond that point, we may be said, in general, to lose more than we gain.

LETTER VIII.

TEMPERANCE.

Πᾶς δὲ ὁ ἀγωνιζόμενος, πάντα ἐγκρατεύεται.—1 *Cor.* ix. 25.

My Dear Sons—You will, perhaps, ask why I devote a whole letter to the subject of temperance, when I have already employed one in relation to morals in general, which might be supposed to include the whole department of duty to which it belongs? I reply, that I regard the subject of strict temperance as so deeply interesting, so vital to the physical well-being, as well as to the moral welfare, and true honour of a student, that I consider no method of making it prominent, and of adding to its impressiveness in this code of counsels, as going beyond its unspeakable importance.

I scarcely ever think of exhorting young men on the subject of temperance, without recollecting an occurrence in my native town, more than half a century ago, which conveyed a lesson to me, at once striking and solemn. A father, who had found a son of eighteen or nineteen years of age, disorderly and unmanageable, proposed to place him under the care and government of a friend at some distance, who had a high reputation for skill and energy in managing disorderly and vicious young men. When the father appeared before this friend with his dissipated and intractable son, he thought himself bound, both in duty and policy, to disclose all the principal faults with which his son was chargeable, without disguise or softening. He began, by saying, "My son is in grain lazy, and cannot be prevailed upon by any influence that I can employ to pursue any occupation." "I am sorry to hear it," said his friend, "but I have been able to reclaim many a youth from habits of inveterate idleness." Again, said the father, "My son is grievously profane, and has given me much distress by his impious language." "That is bad," said the friend, "but I do not despair of curing him of that fault, distressing as it may be." "That is not all," said the father; "he will lie, notwithstanding all that I can do to show him the sin and the disgrace of that practice." "That is, indeed, a dreadful fault," said the friend, "but there is hope of reclaiming him even from that habit, vile and degrading as it undoubtedly is." "I have one more of his faults to mention," said the father. "He has lately manifested a fondness for strong drink, and, when intoxicated, has given me much trouble." "Ah, is it indeed so?" said the friend—"then there is no hope for him! You must take him away. I can do him no good. He will never be cured of that vice." This case actually happened. The result was as predicted. The unhappy young man was taken home again; became more and more sottish; and not long afterwards died a miserable drunkard, the grief and disgrace of his family. And such, I am persuaded, will very seldom fail to be the case with a youthful tippler. Perhaps, indeed, my countryman, in pronouncing concerning the son of his friend, that he would never reform, was rather too prompt and summary in his sentence. I will not say that the recovery of a youth from that vice is in no case to be hoped for. We have reason to be thankful that such a favourable event has sometimes occurred. Nay, among the late triumphs of the temperance cause, we have seen cases of such reformation occurring much more frequently than in former times. Still, of all sinners, I am inclined to think that the lover of intoxicating drinks is among the most hopeless. It is for this reason that I call your attention to the subject of temperance, with all the emphasis and solemnity of which I am capable; and would say, in the language of holy writ—"He that hath ears to hear, let him hear!"

I need not remind you, my dear sons, that the young are peculiarly apt to be ensnared and ruined by stimulating drinks. They are proverbially fond of company and of excitement; having ardent, and too often ungovernable feelings, with little experience, and a proneness to reject the counsels of age and wisdom, no wonder that they are often borne away by the intoxicating draught to insane revelry, to ruinous disorders, and to the wreck of everything good for time and eternity. O, if you had known, as I have, the mischiefs generated in colleges by strong drink; how many amiable and promising young men have been led on from occasional indulgence to abandoned sottishness; and in how many instances young men of polished manners have been betrayed by the stimulus of drink into acts of disorder, and even brutal violence, leading to their temporary suspension from college, and even to their ignominious expulsion, and final ruin, you would not wonder that I speak to you on this subject with so much earnestness and importunity.

You are, no doubt, aware that the laws of the college not only prohibit all intemperate drinking, but that they forbid every student to keep in his room any ardent spirits, or fermented liquors of any kind; and that any such article being found in the room of a student, without permission, is a punishable offence. When you recollect that such a law has been framed and placed in your code by men of wisdom and experience, and that it belongs to the system of all colleges, I am persuaded that you will regard it with approbation, as not at all needlessly strict, and that you will feel bound to obey it to the letter, and with scrupulous care.

Do you not know that all alcoholic and fermented liquors, even those of the mildest form, when taken habitually, or even frequently, excite the nervous system, and thus derange the healthy action of that system; that they injure the tone of the stomach; that they create a craving thirst, which cannot be satisfied without an increase of the same potation which created it; that they slowly but radically, in most cases, affect the liver, and lay the foundation of many loathsome and fatal chronic diseases; that when he who is accustomed to the use of stimulating drinks, in any degree, does become sick, his restoration to health is less probable, and even when it is effected, more slow, because his habit of body interferes with the operation of appropriate remedies, rendering them less active, and, of course, less useful? If you are not aware of all these indubitable facts, it is high time that you should recognize and be convinced of them, and begin that system of entire abstinence from all stimulating drink, which can alone ensure your safety.

Young men are apt to imagine that they are in no danger from this vice. They are each ready to say, with the youthful and inexperienced Syrian of old—"What, is thy servant a dog that he should do this thing?" But there is no vice in the world more alluring, more insidious, or more apt to gain the mastery over those who imagine themselves to be in no danger from its power. Strong drink of any kind excites the feelings. This excitement, by a well-known law of our physical constitution, is, of course, followed by a corresponding nervous depression. This is always more or less painful. A sense of physical want is created. The temptation to recur to the stimulus which produced the preceding excitement will probably be too strong to be resisted. Every successive repetition of the stimulus will increase the craving appetite, and, of course, strengthen the temptation to repeat from day to day the mischievous remedy. Thus have thousands, who never dreamed of being drunkards, been led on from one stage of indulgence to another, as the ox is unconsciously led to the slaughter—"till," as the wise man expresses it—"a dart strikes through his liver, and he knows not that it is for his life." All this, which applies to thousands who scarcely ever read a book, applies with peculiar force to youthful students, who are more apt than others to suffer a depression of animal feeling, and to be betrayed into a love of some artificial excitement.

It ought to be remembered, too, that the indulgence in stimulating drinks is peculiarly injurious to the youthful frame. By this is meant that habits of tippling commenced in early life, are always found to undermine the health, and work their usual mischiefs, more speedily than when the indulgence is commenced in more advanced age. In regard to persons in middle life, and especially those still further advanced, when their bodies have attained more maturity of growth, and firmness of fibre, although the ravages made by stimulating drink are deplorably apparent, and finally fatal; yet it is observable that the human frame, under these ravages, bears up longer, and seems harder to be vanquished than in the more youthful subject. This is more tender, more excitable, more easily deranged, and, of course, more speedily prostrated, than the aged frame. Accordingly, it has been remarked, by experienced, sagacious observers, that when a young person of eighteen or twenty years of age begins to indulge, even in a small degree, in strong drink, his bodily strength is soon undermined, and he commonly falls an early prey to the destroyer.

Listen, then, my dear sons, to an affectionate father, when, with all that earnestness which long experience and deep conviction warrant, he entreats you to eschew and avoid all use whatever of stimulating drinks. Touch nothing of the kind as an ordinary beverage. Drink nothing but water, and you will be the better for it as long as you live. I believe that intoxicating drinks do not help, but injure nine hundred and ninety-nine out of every thousand of those who use them; and that their entire banishment from literary institutions is so unspeakably desirable, that it is better—far better that the thousandth person should suffer a little for want of them, than that their disuse in all colleges should not be complete.

These being my views, it has given me great pleasure to learn, that a society has been formed in your college, embracing the pledge of "total abstinence from all that can intoxicate." I know that some, both in and out of college, consider this as a fanatical extreme, and set their faces against it. This is not my opinion. I am persuaded that temperance societies, on the "total abstinence" plan, have done much good, and are likely to do much more. What though they have been carried on by agents of suspicious character, and recommended by arguments of a worse than suspicious kind? The best things have been perverted, but ought not, on that account, to be disused. It is my earnest advice, therefore, that you should become members of the society alluded to, and not only adhere to its pledge with sacred fidelity, but endeavour to promote its popularity and influence by all the means in your power. True, indeed, some of the advocates of "total abstinence" urge their doctrine by arguments, which I can by no means sustain. They tell us that the word of God gives no countenance to the use of fermented wine, in any case whatever, and that it is not lawful to use such wine at the Lord's table. In these positions I cannot concur. They appear to me unscriptural, and in respect to the Lord's Supper, directly to set at defiance the Saviour's express command. I can never believe, that he instituted an ordinance, the tendency of which is to make men drunkards. Still, so far as the advocates of the doctrine in question come to the practical result, that all persons in health ought to abstain from all intoxicating drink, as an ordinary beverage, for the promotion of their own well-being, and on the principle of expediency, for discouraging their use by others, I am cordially with them, and sincerely wish that all college students in the land were banded in such associations.

You know that I never set any alcoholic or fermented liquors on my own table. This has been my practice for many years; and I have adopted the practice from a conscientious persuasion that my own health, and that of all my family is benefited by it; and also from an earnest desire to promote, by my example, the banishment of all such drinks from all classes of society. When I see so many around me, young and old, falling victims to the use of such drinks; and especially when I see so many young men of the finest minds, and devoted to literary pursuits, led astray, and some of them finally ruined in body and mind by this deceiver, can you wonder that I am unable to restrain my pen when the subject is in question? Can you consider any zeal as excessive, which contemplates the banishment of intoxicating drinks in every form from the precincts of our literary institutions? As a friend to my species, I feel constrained to do all in my power, to discourage the use of this insidious poison. It is no sacrifice to me to abstain from all intoxicating drinks myself. On the contrary, my firm persuasion is, that, by this abstinence, I promote my own present enjoyment, and that of my children. But even if it were otherwise, I should feel myself abundantly rewarded for the sacrifice, by the consciousness of pursuing a course adapted to discourage and diminish the use of one of the most destructive agents that ever cursed the human family. And if I can prevail on my children to enter into the spirit of this principle, and not only to begin, in the morning of life, to restrain their own appetites, but also to co-operate cordially in a plan for the benefit of others, it will afford me unspeakable gratification, as a pledge that they will prove benefactors to the world.

If you desire, my dear sons, to avoid the degrading snare of stimulating drinks, avoid, I beseech you, all the company which will be likely to lead to it. Intemperance is, generally, and especially in its beginnings, a social vice. As "one sinner," in all the walks of life, "destroys much good;" so it is eminently true, that one votary of this kind of excitement can hardly fail of endangering the virtue of others. Fly from the society of all such as you would from the most deadly plague. If you know of any room in which stimulating drink of any kind is kept, avoid it as you would the room of a counterfeiter, or receiver of stolen goods. If you enter it, none can tell what may be the consequence. Even if you should not be tempted to partake of the interdicted draught, who can assure you that your character may not be unexpectedly implicated by your being found or seen in the infected region?

In fact, any student of college who finds the stimulus of company necessary to his comfort, ought to consider himself as on the verge of a fatal gulf. He who cannot be comfortable in the retirement of his study; who does not feel the acquirement of knowledge a rich gratification, but finds the excitement of company, and the social song indispensable to his enjoyment, has the most reason to be alarmed for his safety. The vital principle of intemperance has already taken up its abode in his person, and without a miracle, will probably make him its victim.

I should be utterly ashamed, my dear sons, to plead so much at length, a cause so plain, and so manifestly important, and indeed vital, as that of temperance, were it not that, after all, some young men are so infatuated, nay so suicidal as to disregard all warning, and plunge into the gulf of infamy and perdition, in sight of the many beacons erected to guard them against it. Every one who has eyes to see, perceives that, when young men, under the excitement of company, have intoxicating drink within their reach, they will seldom fail to abuse it. Every one is forced to acknowledge that nine-tenths of all the disorders and crimes in colleges, as well as in the civil community, arise directly or indirectly from the excitement of inebriating liquors; and yet young men, who claim to have both talents and moral principle, are neither afraid nor ashamed to seek the intoxicating cup, and feel as if they had gained a triumph when they can enjoy the privilege of making brutes of themselves!

I will add here, that if you wish to avoid the gulf of intemperance, you must by all means avoid the use of tobacco in any form. There are few things more adapted to inspire disgust on the score of manners, or deep apprehension for the future welfare of young men, than to see them puffing their cigars in the faces of all who approach them, or chewing their nauseous quids, and squirting their filthy saliva in every direction. The mischiefs wrought on the human system by this narcotic weed, are so many and serious, that the only wonder is, that any intelligent young man, who does not wish to court disease and danger should allow himself to use it. I do not say that every one who uses it incurs the mischiefs to which I refer; but I assert that every one is in danger of incurring them, and that if he escapes, it is not owing to any want of evil tendency in the indulgence itself, but to the favour of a merciful Providence. There can be no doubt that both chewing and smoking tobacco, especially the former, have been the means of making thousands of drunkards.

Do you ask what connection exists between the use of tobacco and the habit of intemperance in drinking? I answer, great every way. Do you not know that that filthy and pernicious weed, when either chewed or smoked, is a strong exciter of the nervous system; and that, of course, it deranges the natural and healthful action of that system? Do you not know that it impairs the appetite; that it interferes with the regular digestion of food; that it often induces distressing and incurable diseases, not only of the stomach, but also of the whole body? Are you not aware that the progress of morbid habit in the use of tobacco, is exactly the same as in the use of spirituous liquors? The slaves of it begin with what they call the temperate, and even sparing, use of the article. They take, perhaps, a single cigar, or a single quid, or a single pinch of snuff, in a given number of hours. But, after a while, the appetite for this indulgence is ever craving and never satisfied; the sensibility of the body of course diminishes with the increase of the frequency and quantity of the stimulus; until, at last, the miserable individual is wretched without it; and when he cannot obtain the indulgence, is reduced to a state of suffering more distressing than when tortured by the most importunate hunger. I have often known persons, when deprived of the use of tobacco for a few hours, wholly unfit for either study or conversation, and thrown into a state of agitation but little short of mental derangement. Is it wise in any one to create such an artificial craving as may make him the sport of circumstances, and the absence of a paltry indulgence destructive to his comfort, and even, for a time, to his usefulness?

It has been said, indeed, that chewing and smoking tobacco, assist the operations of the mind; that they produce a soothing and quickening influence which is friendly to study, and especially to all works of composition and eloquence. But do not ardent spirits and wine give insidious aid of the same kind; and is not the ultimate effect, in both cases, deceptive and often fatal?

Nor is the tendency of tobacco less obvious to produce ultimate intemperance in the use of distilled and fermented liquors. One of the usual effects of smoking and chewing is thirst. This thirst cannot be allayed by water; for no insipid beverage will be relished when the mouth and throat have been exposed to the stimulus of the smoke or juice of tobacco. A desire is, of course, excited for strong drink; and this, when taken between meals, will soon lead to habits of intoxication. I have seen so many chewers and smokers ensnared into the inordinate love of inebriating drinks, that I always tremble when I see any one, and especially a young person, becoming fond of the cigar or the quid, and consider him as on the verge of a precipice.

I have forborne to say anything of the enormous expense of smoking, especially as this indulgence is conducted by some students of reckless habits. I cannot doubt that some members of colleges have added one hundred dollars a year to the other charges of their education, for this hateful and offensive indulgence alone; in a few cases perhaps double that sum. How a young man of reflection has been able to settle such an account with his own conscience, and with an affectionate parent, who was, perhaps, denying himself for the sake of furnishing the requisite funds for a beloved son, I know not. I am constrained to think less of the moral sentiments, as well as of the understanding, of one who is capable of reconciling himself to such extravagance for so hateful and injurious a purpose.

My opposition to the use of tobacco in the form of snuff is scarcely less decisive than that to the other forms of this noxious weed. The effects of snuff in affecting the voice, the complexion, and the nervous system, are well known to all persons of much observation. I have seen deplorable cases of nasal obstruction, of nervous tremulousness, and various forms of disease induced by this disgusting habit; and every young person who indulges in it in any degree, is in danger of being led on by degrees, until he shall become a distress to himself, and an offence to all who approach him.

Let me entreat you, then, my dear sons, never to indulge in the use of tobacco in any form, or in any degree. Whether the temptation assail you by assuming the guise of a remedy for some disease, or as a source of social enjoyment, believe not its promises. It is a deceiver, and will, sooner or later, give reason for repentance.

The late Dr. Franklin, a few months before his death, declared to a friend, that he had never used tobacco in any way in the course of a long life ; and that one striking fact had exerted much influence on his mind in relation to this practice, viz : that he never had met with any one who was addicted to the use of it who advised him to follow his example. I will add to this statement another of similar and still more decisive import. I never yet met with a large consumer of tobacco in any form, who, when interrogated on the subject, did not say, that if he had to live his life over again, he would avoid the habit which had made him its slave ; and that he would by no means advise his children to do as he had done.

I expressed an opinion, on a preceding page, that you ought to make water your only common beverage. My own personal experience, as well as close observation on the habits of others, convince me of the wisdom of this advice. If you wish to live out all your days, and to possess a sound mind in a sound body, drink nothing else, as a habit. But you may drink too much, even of water. The habit of incessantly guzzling even this simple and innocent fluid, either marks the existence of disease, or will probably lead to it. It indicates the presence, or the approach of a feverish diathesis ; or if it do not spring from the power of disease already formed, it will be likely, by deluging the stomach with fluid, by diluting the gastric juice, and thus impairing its appropriate power, to interfere with digestion, and, of course, to impair the health. Thirst is quite as well slaked, in my experience, by two or three spoonfuls as by a pint or a quart ; and all beyond this moderate portion tends rather to load the stomach than to refresh and nourish. The habit of flooding the stomach with fluids is, undoubtedly, to most people, very injurious. The drier our food when we receive it the better. At least all my observation leads me so to pronounce.

Besides, if I mistake not, I have had occasion to remark, that the habit of intemperance in drinking even water is apt ultimately to betray those who indulge it, into the intemperate use of intoxicating drinks. Where persons find perpetual drinking necessary to their comfort; where they have induced a constant artificial thirst, and are continually moistening their lips and fauces with the mildest fluid; what can be more natural than gradually to slide into the use of something more sapid and stimulating? The incessant drinker will seldom be long together satisfied with water alone.

LETTER IX.

THE FORMATION AND THE VALUE OF CHARACTER.

"Whatsoever things are true, whatsoever things are honest, whatsoever things are just, whatsoever things are pure, whatsoever things are lovely, whatsoever things are of good report; if there be any virtue, and if there be any praise, think on these things."—PHILIP. iv. 8.

MY DEAR SONS—I take for granted that you have a laudable desire to maintain an elevated character, not only among your fellow students, but also in general society, and throughout life. I have no objection to styling this desire a commendable ambition. I am aware that the term ambition is generally used in a bad sense, and that it is not commonly numbered among the Christian virtues. But I am unwilling that the devil should appropriate such an expressive and convenient word to his own use. Ambition may be groveling and criminal, or it may be elevated and noble. It is always the latter when its object is the attainment of true excellence, and the enjoyment of high esteem among the wise and the good. The Latin scholar will immediately trace its etymology to the practice among the old Romans, of candidates for office "going about" to solicit the good opinion and votes of the people. But when any one seeks to excel in virtuous and useful conduct; when he desires to have a "good name" among his fellow men; and for the attainment of this, among higher and better objects, "goes about" doing good—seeking to promote the welfare of all around him;—who will hesitate to say, that this is a laudable ambition? The truth is, this feeling, like the desire of happiness, is good or evil according to the direction which it takes, and the means which it employs. I indulge the hope that the ambition of my beloved sons will be neither irregular nor ignoble; but will have for its object that "good name which is rather to be chosen than great riches, and that loving favour which is more precious than silver or gold."

Ask yourselves, then, what is that thing called elevated character, which is most highly esteemed among wise men, and which is most worthy of your pursuit? It is not the possession of great wealth. Some of the richest men that ever lived have been among the most vile and detestable. The great Governor of the world often testifies "of how little value exorbitant wealth is in his sight, by bestowing it upon the most unworthy of mortals."* Neither does the character of which I speak consist of great popularity among the multitude. This popularity has frequently been attained, and sometimes in a very high degree, by men who were destitute of a single virtue, and who ought to have been universally abhorred. Nor does it necessarily imply great genius, or intellectual powers of a very high order. These endowments fall to the lot of very few men, and even these are sometimes monsters of wickedness. What wise man would be willing to take the talents of Byron, at the expense of incurring his moral infamy? On the contrary, some of the most beloved and useful men that ever lived, did not possess extraordinary talents, but that happy combination of good sense, sound judgment, and great moral purity and activity, which fitted them to be a blessing to mankind.

What, then, is that character which is most highly esteemed by the wise and the good; which most certainly and effectually commands public esteem and confidence; and which a man of really elevated views would wish to enjoy? No thinking person can be for a moment at a loss to answer this question. It is a

* Arbuthnot's Epitaph on *Francis Chartres.*

character which exhibits the combined and noble qualities of respectable talents, sound and extensive knowledge, immovable integrity and honour, persevering industry in every laudable pursuit, fidelity to every engagement, enlightened, steady patriotism, a spirit of warm, diffusive, active benevolence, and unfeigned consistent piety. Where these qualities meet and shine in any individual—and the more complete the assemblage the better—all parties will unite in ascribing to him an exalted character; all will concur in saying—this is the "highest style of man." Even the vilest profligate in the community would earnestly desire, if it were possible, to possess such a character; and if he were about to select a medical attendant for his family, in severe sickness; a legal counsellor for himself, in a case of important and perplexing controversy; an executor of his estate, or a guardian for his children; he would say, with instinctive eagerness, "Give me a man not only of sound talents and knowledge, but also of high and unblemished moral and religious character." Even atheists have never failed to prefer such men for important confidential trusts, to those of their own class. And why is it thus? simply because the character which I have described, is best adapted to prepare those who possess it, to meet all the relations, to perform all the duties, and to enjoy all the comforts of life, and to promote the welfare and happiness of all around them.

The value of such a character, as a commodity in the market, is inestimable. The qualities, indeed, which go to form such a character are intrinsically excellent, and ought to be prized for their own sake. But their value does not end here. They elevate their possessor in public estimation. They inspire confidence not only, as I have said, on the part of the wise and the good, but of all classes of society. They put it in his power to take a higher professional stand; to command larger emoluments for his services; and, in short, to attain honours and rewards in proportion to their popular acceptance.

Now, if such be the character which is most truly desirable; which is most esteemed by all classes of men; which is the richest source of influence and power; and which is adapted to secure the greatest amount both of usefulness and enjoyment,—surely every one who is preparing to live, should keep this object continually in view, and seek its attainment as the best earthly treasure. He cannot begin too early, or labour too diligently, to gain that which is unspeakably more precious than all the stores of mammon that were ever amassed. On the one hand, whatever else a man may gain, if his character be not elevated, he is poor indeed; and, on the other hand, whatever he may lose, if his character be untarnished and high, he is still rich. Friends may die; wealth may take to itself wings and fly away; honourable office may be wrested from him; but if his character remain unsullied, his most precious earthly possession is still left him; he can still call his own all that love, respect, and true honour, which may enable him either to regain all that he has lost, or to live contented and happy without it.

This being the case, it has often excited in my mind great surprise, and not a little regret, to find members of college, not freshmen merely, but juniors, and even seniors, apparently taking no thought for the establishment of a high and honourable character among their fellow students, and the mass of their acquaintances. I see them indulging a temper, using language, exhibiting manners, and allowing themselves to pursue a system of conduct, adapted to excite the aversion and distrust, if not the utter enmity, of all who are connected with them. Surely such young men forget that, even if they succeed in becoming eminent scholars, it will only be to render themselves more conspicuously odious, and, of course, more unable to rise in the world; and they equally forget, that if it be desirable and important that a good character be formed, as it is not the growth of a day, or of a sudden volition, the sooner they begin to form and to build it up the better.

This character, let it ever be remembered, must in all cases be formed by the individual himself. I do not mean, of course, by this remark, to exclude that divine aid by which everything truly good in our hearts or lives is attained. Without that aid we can do nothing. But my meaning is, that every one's character depends on the spirit and conduct which he himself possesses and exhibits. He cannot leave to others the task of forming it for him, any more than he can leave to others the task of eating, and drinking, and breathing to sustain his life. His own spirit and acts must form his character. It is not enough that the parents or other relatives of a young man maintain a high standing. They may occupy the very highest position in office, honour and wealth that can possibly be enjoyed; but if he have no character of his own, these advantages will be so far from sustaining him, that their influence will be rather adverse in its nature. His degradation will assuredly be, by contrast, more complete, in public estimation, on account of the other members of his family. I have known not a few young men evidently ruined, by acting on the presumption that the character of their parents would sustain them, without effort on their part, and who, under this impression, neglected the cultivation of their minds, and took no pains to form virtuous habits, or to establish a reputation of their own. Never was there a more deplorable mistake than this. Character is a personal matter. It must be strictly your own, or it can profit you nothing. There is a sense, and that a most important one, in which it may be said, that all the world cannot sustain your reputation, if you neglect it yourselves. It must, under God, be constantly sustained by yourselves, or it will fall into ruin.

So far as my observation has gone, the greater part of college students appear to have no laudable emulation at all. They are sunk in intellectual and moral apathy, neither aiming nor striving to excel in anything. And when a few are roused to a measure of zeal and effort, their desire seems to be directed to mere excellence in scholarship, and nothing else. If they can outstrip all others in study and attainments, their utmost wishes are answered. This is, no doubt, an important part of the character which ought to be sought by every young man; but it is not the whole, nay, it is not the most essential part. Many a youth has gained the "first honour," who had a hateful temper, and never attained any high degree of esteem among men, notwithstanding his mere literary triumph. It is my earnest desire, my dear sons, that you may acquire and maintain a character for eminent scholarship; but it would grieve me to the heart if your character went no further than this. My still more ardent desire is, that you may attain and manifest all those moral and religious qualities which excite esteem, which command confidence, which secure the love of the wise and the good, and which prepare for eminent usefulness. This, this is the character which, in prosperity and adversity, in sickness and in health, in sorrow and in joy, in life and in death, will bear its possessor through, and never fail him.

Allow me to say, further, that I desire for you that decision of character which is adapted to resist all temptation, and to overbear every unfriendly influence. The great unhappiness of many, and especially of many young men, is that, though their principles are correct, and their intentions good, they are apt to yield to solicitation. They cannot put a decisive negative on the wishes and entreaties of beloved friends. This is a deplorable weakness, which has led to many a false step, and to many a shipwreck of youthful promise. It is one of the most precious attainments of a young man, not only to be established in good principles, but to have them so fixed, firm, and governing, as to stand equally unmoved against the terrors of menace, and the enticements of flattery; to cultivate a firmness of moral purpose which dares to deny, and which is not ashamed, in pursuing the path of duty, to put custom, fashion, and the solicitation of the greatest numbers at defiance. This moral courage, boldness, and decision, impart a finish to a character in all other respects good, which is at once as ornamental as it is useful.

While I call upon you to consider the importance of character, and to recollect that it is a treasure to be formed and maintained by yourselves; I would, at the same time, remind you that it is a most delicate thing, which a single false step may irretrievably destroy. Young men are apt, indeed, to imagine that their conduct during the period of adolescence is of small importance. They admit, and perhaps in some measure feel, that, by and by, when they shall have advanced a little further in the career of life, every step that they take will be practically momentous. They allow that reputation then will be, indeed, a tender plant, easily blasted, and requiring to be protected and nurtured with the utmost care. But now they imagine that they may take considerable liberties with their reputation; that juvenile mistakes, and even serious delinquencies, will be readily overlooked and soon forgotten by an indulgent community. There never was a greater mistake. All my experience leads me to say, that the aberrations of college students from the paths of integrity and honour, are remembered against them with a degree of tenacity and permanency truly instructive. I have known one false step in college, one dishonest or dishonourable action, one consent, in an evil hour, to become a partaker in a disreputable scheme or enterprise, to fasten itself upon a young man, to follow him, and to adhere to him to his dying day. I could easily specify examples, if it were proper, of gross lying, petty theft, mean deception, or swindling, which occurred in different colleges, at eighteen or nineteen years of age, which no subsequent conduct could ever obliterate from the popular memory; which followed their perpetrators through a long public career; and which some coarse rival or opponent brought up to their confusion and shame in old age. When will the wretch, who, not long since, murdered Professor Davis, of the University of Virginia, be able to escape from the infamy, and if he be not a fiend incarnate, from the remorse, of that awful crime? Even if, by the grace of God, he were to become a saint from this hour, how would he obtain deliverance from the tortures of his own mind, or from the reproaches of every one who identified his person, though taking refuge in the remotest corner of the globe to which his flight may bear him?

Let me say, then, my dear sons, if you desire to form and maintain an honourable character through life, begin now to establish it, to watch over it, to guard with the utmost care against everything that can, by possibility, affect it unfavourably. Try to establish a reputation with all with whom you have intercourse, for a strict regard to truth, and for the most scrupulous adherence to integrity and honour in every transaction. Let nothing tempt you to engage, for a moment, in any scheme or enterprise involving duplicity, underhand dealing, or anything that could tempt you to shun the light. Allow yourselves to deceive nobody. Enter into no cabal. Put it into no one's power to charge you with a mean trick, or double dealing, in the smallest concern. Rather suffer anything yourselves than deceive, betray, or injure any human being. Let no false shame, no fear of giving offence, no desire to conciliate friends, ever tempt you to consent to that which your judgment condemns. Dare to do what your conscience tells you is right—whomsoever it may disappoint or offend. Avoid with sacred care slander, backbiting, in short, everything inconsistent with the strictest justice, the most elevated magnanimity, and the purest benevolence. Never indulge that gossiping spirit, which leads to the propagation, however honestly, of evil reports, and which frequently involves those who indulge it in vexatious and not very honourable explanations and apologies. You are preparing, if permitted to live, for public usefulness. For such a life, in any profession, a degree of reserve, caution, and even taciturnity, is indispensable. Begin now that self-discipline which will prepare you for all the solemn and delicate responsibilities of public station. A man "full of talk" will often find himself embarrassed by the unbridled effusions of his own tongue. "Be swift to hear, slow to speak, slow to wrath." In a word, let it be your aim in everything, to establish such a character as shall compel every one who knows you, to rely on your word as much as upon other men's oaths; and to say, whenever there is occasion to speak of you, "Here, if anywhere on earth, we shall find candour, truth and honour."

LETTER X.

PATRIOTISM.

"Pro Patria, Pro Patria."

My Dear Sons—An eastern sage was wont to say, "No life is pleasing to God, that is not useful to man." The spirit of Christianity still more clearly and strongly inculcates the same sentiment. The Saviour constantly "went about doing good." His daily walks, and all his miracles had for their object the instruction of the ignorant, the relief of suffering, and the promotion of the temporal and eternal welfare of men.

This is the pattern for all who profess to be his disciples. Nay more, it is not only the pattern presented and recommended to the Christian, but it is a plan of living so reasonable, so beautiful, so wise, and so attractive in itself, that every rational creature ought to make it his model. It were an easy task, independently of revelation, to demonstrate that such a life, on the part of every social being, is demanded by his own true interest, and by the happiness of society, as well as by the authority of God. It is true on the real principles of natural religion, as well as of revealed, that no man can innocently live to himself.

What ingenuous youthful student of the classics has not felt a generous ardour glowing in his bosom, when he dwelt on that oft repeated maxim of the pagan poet, "*Dulce et decorum est pro patria mori;*" and when he read of the self-sacrifices of Curtius, and of the Decii, father, son and grandson, for the sake of their country? Surely these feelings are not kindled by an ideal abstraction!

I am aware that it has been said, that we nowhere find patriotism enjoined as a virtue in the Christian Scriptures. And if by patriotism be meant, as some understand the term to mean, that exclusive or paramount attachment to a particular nation, because we happen to be members of it, which permits us to disregard the rights or invade the interests of other nations; then, indeed, the word of God neither enjoins nor allows it. The religion of the Bible is adapted and intended for all nations alike. And, of course, the spirit of the Bible is a spirit of universal benevolence, which desires and aims to promote the welfare of every creature.

We are not, indeed, to consider Christianity as teaching that we are to have no more regard for our own country than for any other. Such a view of duty would be unnatural, and likely to exert, in the end, a mischievous influence. The apostle Paul expresses, in Rom. ix. 3, a special attachment to "his brethren, his kinsmen, according to the flesh;" and the same inspired man still more strongly and solemnly expresses the same sentiment, when he says, 1 Tim. v. 8, "He that provideth not for his own, and especially for those of his own house, hath denied the faith, and is worse than an infidel." The truth is, it is always most natural and most easy to consult the interest and promote the welfare of those among whom we dwell, to whom we can have ready access, and especially who are cast upon our care. It would, indeed, be superlatively absurd to leave our own children to the care of strangers, while we took care of theirs; or to leave the concerns of our own country to be looked after and managed by foreigners, while we undertook to legislate and judge for other countries. Nevertheless, though our own families, our own towns, and our own country, ought to engage far more of our attention and care than other families, other towns, and other countries, yet we are not at liberty so to care for ourselves as to disregard or oppose the welfare of others. But while we are peculiarly careful to do good to our own, we are quite as carefully to avoid all invasion of the rights or happiness of other families or nations.

Dr. Johnson, indeed, once said, that "patriotism is the last refuge of a scoundrel." By this apothegm that eminent man did not mean to say, that there is no such genuine virtue; but that, in ninety-nine cases out of an hundred, its most forward and noisy claimants were supremely and dishonestly selfish, and really seeking their own aggrandizement, not their country's welfare. This witness is true. There can be no doubt that the greater number of those who claim for their zeal and their toil the patriot's name, are actuated by the meanest selfishness, and are seeking nothing but their own advantage. Yet, sordid and base as the greater portion of those who take this name are, patriotism is not a mere name. It is a precious reality. And I wish you to possess it.

He is the truest patriot, then, in the Christian sense of the word, who loves his own country with sincere peculiar affection, and constantly labours to promote her true honour and happiness, but without injuring or diminishing the welfare of any other country; who devotes his time, his counsels, and his best efforts, for bestowing intellectual, moral, and physical benefits on the community to which he belongs; but at the same time desires and strives to bestow the same benefits, as far as may be, on all other communities. In short, Christian patriotism considers nothing as foreign from its care which tends to promote the happiness of man; and for this purpose plans and labours, first to confer all possible benefits on its own family and nation, and then on other families and nations to the remotest bounds of human society. In a word, the spirit of genuine patriotism is the spirit which prompts to do good in every way to every branch of the human family, and especially to those with whom we are more immediately connected, or who are placed most directly within our reach. This is the noble virtue which I should be glad to see my sons cultivating, and which I hope will more and more shine in them as long as they live.

A venerable English reformer, nearly three centuries ago, when he was drawing near the close of life, exclaimed with emphasis, "*Pro Ecclesia Dei; Pro Ecclesia Dei!*" It would gratify me more than I can express to know that similar language, whether in sickness or in health, in life or in death, was constantly uppermost on your lips. But it would also afford me high pleasure to know that, even now, in the walks of the college, your minds are animated with a noble ambition to discharge with fidelity all your duties as good citizens, and that in looking forward to your course in life, you often have in your minds the spirit, and on your lips the language of the motto, which stands at the head of this letter—*Pro Patria—Pro Patria!*

Perhaps you are ready to say, that a letter on patriotism is hardly appropriate in a code of counsels addressed to lads in college; that advice on such a topic would bé more seasonable if intended for young men entering on professional life, and preparing to discharge their duties as active citizens. If such a thought arise in your minds, it indicates immature conceptions of the subject. The present is your seed-time of life, not only in regard to the acquisition of knowledge, but also in respect to the sentiments and habits of thinking which are to stamp your whole course. Alexander Hamilton, the first Secretary of the Treasury of the United States, came to this country, a youth of sixteen, a short time before the crisis of our contest with Great Britain, and the commencement of the revolutionary war. Though this was only his adopted country, yet, as he resolved to cast in his lot with her, he soon began to feel that she had claims upon him, and that his best powers ought to be devoted to her service. Even while he was in college, his patriotic zeal was awakened to plead her cause, and endeavour to promote her welfare. At that early period he wrote a number of pieces in the journals of the day, in favour of independence, so judicious, so eloquent, and in every respect so elevated in their character, that they were, at first, ascribed to the pen of one of the ablest writers and statesmen of New York. With what ardour, ability and usefulness the subsequent portions of his life were devoted to the service of his country, in her armies, her deliberative bodies, and her cabinet, no one who is acquainted with our history is ignorant.

This example, and many others which might be cited, both in this country and the land of our fathers, show that the sooner you begin to realize to yourselves that your country has a claim on you, and that you are bound to respond to that claim by preparing to serve her with your best powers, the better. Such a practical impression, recognized and carried out into habitual act, is adapted to exert an influence on the whole character of a young man, of the happiest kind.

It cannot fail to enlarge and elevate his mind. One of the greatest faults of most young men is, that their views are narrow and sordid. They do not lift their minds to high and remote objects. If their present appetites and wishes can be gratified; if their present little tasks can be acceptably performed, it is enough. They look for no preparation, recognize no responsibility beyond this. But the moment the principle of genuine patriotism takes root, and springs up in the mind, it presents an object of desire, a motive to action, at once noble and elevating. It carries its possessor out of himself, and disposes him to make sacrifices to principle. The youth begins to see that he is bound to live for a great purpose. His country, in consequence of his connecting with it his own destiny, appears more precious. He cherishes a sacred emulation to be a benefactor to the community and to the world. He desires that the world may be the better and happier for his having lived in it. He, of course, shapes his plans, his studies, and his habits accordingly. He cultivates his powers, stores his mind with knowledge, and labours to attain that species of excellence which will enable him most effectually to serve the public. In short, the mind of such a youth is cast, as it were, into a mould adapted to great attainments, great services, and great usefulness.

Such a youth will, of course, learn to see and despise that noisy, heartless pretension to patriotism, which flows, not from the least love of country, but from a desire to make a living out of the country, or to be decorated with her honours. This, it is to be feared, is the real spirit of nine-tenths, if not much more, of all the professed patriotism which is most ardent and obtrusive. This spirit is indeed, what the great English moralist styles it, "the last refuge of a scoundrel." The young patriot in college will have made no small acquisition, when he has learned the sordid, despicable character of this spirit, and acquired a real taste for something higher and better.

I need scarcely add, that the student who has imbibed something of the patriotic spirit, will not be found lending his aid, or even his countenance, to any species of disorder in college. He will regard perfect obedience to the laws as an essential part of the character, not only of a good student, but also of a good citizen. He will turn away, upon principle, from all the practices which are unfriendly to order, to purity, to health, and, in general, to the best interests of society. He will refuse to employ his time in reading books, whatever may be their fascinations, which are immoral, and, of course, mischievous in their tendency. In a word, he will abhor everything which is unfriendly to the happiness of the community; and will grudge no toil which is adapted to put him in possession of any knowledge or accomplishment, by which he may be better qualified to become an ornament and a benefactor to his country.

I hope, my dear sons, you will no longer say or think, that this is a subject on which it is unsuitable to address a student in college. So far from this being, in my estimation, the case, I am constrained to say, that, next to the piety of the heart, which is, more than anything else, the anchor of the soul, and better adapted to hold it fast, and to hold it comfortably on the troubled ocean of life—I desire my sons to imbibe the spirit of patriotism; to feel that they belong to their country, as well as their God, and that they are solemnly bound to cultivate every power, and to make every attainment, which will qualify them to be so many sources of light, and virtue, and happiness to the community. Because I know that the more deeply this principle shall take root in their minds, the more benign the influence which it will exert over the whole character. Such a principle will not be a mere name. It will sober the mind. It will impress a deep sense of responsibility. It will excite to diligence in study. It will guard a young man against giving his time to that frivolous or mischievous reading, which tends to his injury, instead of preparing him for the duties of practical life. In short, it will tend to impart that sobriety, that dignity, that industry, that desire to serve his generation, and that desire to live in the affections, and in the memory of his fellow citizens, which we may hope will be the means of preparing him to be the man, and to make the attainments, which are the objects of his noble ambition.

LETTER XI.

PARTICULAR STUDIES.

Floriferis ut apes in saltibus omnia libant,
Omnia nos itidem depascimur aurea dicta.—LUCRETIUS.

MY DEAR SONS—When some one asked Agesilaus, the king of Sparta, what it was in which youth ought principally to be instructed, he very wisely replied, "That which they will have most need to practise when they are men." I said that this was a wise reply; and so it undoubtedly was, if we could assume that every one knows in youth what he may have most occasion for when he becomes a man. But I contend that no man knows what the providence of God has in reserve for him in after life; and, of course, no one can tell, in all cases, what branch of knowledge, among those which he is called to study, may be of most importance to him hereafter, either as a means of subsistence, or as an avenue to honour and usefulness. If, therefore, a student of college were to ask me, "Which of my prescribed studies shall I attend to with diligence?" I would certainly reply—"to all; neglect none of them—be not content to be superficial in any of them. It may be that, in after life, you may find those branches of knowledge, which you are now tempted to undervalue, of more vital importance to you than all the rest put together. To meet an exigency of this kind, try to be thorough in every study; and then you may be prepared for any situation in which the providence of God may place you.

I shall never forget a remarkable example, which at

once illustrates and confirms this advice. I was intimately acquainted, in early life, with one of the most accomplished scholars our country ever bred. I refer to the Rev. Dr. John Ewing, of Philadelphia, for many years Provost—another name for President—of the University of Pennsylvania. He was a graduate of the College of New Jersey, which then had its location in Newark, but now in Princeton. He belonged to the class which was graduated in 1755, and, after reading what I am about to state, you will not wonder that he was greatly distinguished in his class. He remarked, one day, in my hearing, that in the earlier stages of his college life, he was often tempted to slight what he then deemed some of the less essential branches of his prescribed course. He sometimes, he said, asked himself, "Of what use can some of these studies possibly be to me in after life?" Partly by his own better reflections, however, and partly by the advice of the venerable President Burr, then at the head of the institution, he was induced neither to neglect nor slight any study, under the impression that he might have occasion for them all in his subsequent course. This suggestion, which he contemplated as a possibility, was amply realized. After the lapse of a few years, he was himself placed at the head of an important college, and found abundant use for all his acquirements. He was probably more thoroughly accomplished in all the branches of knowledge usually studied in the best colleges, than any other native American of his day; and probably few of his contemporaries in any country exceeded him. This qualified him not only to maintain an enlightened superintendence over the whole institution committed to his care, but also enabled him in the occasional absence of any professor, whatever his branch of instruction might be, to take his place, at a moment's warning, and perform his duties quite as well as the professor himself. This he was often known to do, to the admiration of circles of waiting pupils, who saw no other difference between him and their regular professor in that branch, than a manifest superiority of taste, accuracy, and profundity on the part of their accomplished president.

Nor is this by any means the only example which experience has furnished of the vital importance to individuals of diligence and faithfulness in pursuing every branch of their collegiate course. On the one hand, I have known a number of graduates of colleges, who, though in affluent circumstances at the time of their graduation, were unexpectedly reduced to poverty, who found the genuine and ripe scholarship which they had been wise enough to acquire in college, a source of ample and honourable support as long as they lived. On the other hand, I have know many examples of young men who, with the best opportunities, were lazy enough, or inconsiderate enough, to make all their studies slight and superficial, and who afterwards found, to their mortification and loss, that they had not scholarship sufficient to qualify them for any of the situations to which they might otherwise have aspired, and which would have secured them both comfort and honour.

I entreat you, then, my dear sons, not to cheat yourselves in regard to this matter. For, truly, every young man may be said to cheat himself, more than he cheats his teachers or his guardians, when he slights or neglects the study of any important branch of knowledge which belongs to a liberal education. By so doing, he diminishes his own treasures, and lessens his own power, both of doing good, and of obtaining pre-eminence in life. The more you can store your minds, with every species of useful knowledge, the better prepared you will be to "serve your generation by the will of God," and to attain that true honour among men, which the union of knowledge and virtue never fails to secure.

But, notwithstanding this general principle, which ought to govern every student, it cannot be doubted that there are some branches of knowledge more radical in their value and influence than others, and which, therefore, ought to be cultivated with peculiar zeal and diligence. If, therefore, you ask me, which of all the studies prescribed in your collegiate course, you ought to regard with especial favour, and to cultivate with special preference and labour, I would, without the least hesitation, say they are the ancient languages and Mathematics. Study to be at home in all the branches prescribed for your course; but in these make a point of being strong, mature, and rich. If you should be compelled, by feeble health, or by any other consideration, to pass more hastily than you could wish over any particular studies, let neither of these two be of the number. They are fundamental in all intellectual culture, and, when in any good degree mastered, diffuse an influence over all the other departments of knowledge which every good scholar will perceive, and which none but a good scholar can appreciate.

You are aware that some of the friends of liberal knowledge in general, have laboured hard to depress the claims of classical literature, as an indispensable part even of a collegial course of study. But the longer I reflect on the subject, the deeper is my conviction that all such efforts are the result either of ignorance, or of that deplorable infatuation which is sometimes found to enslave the minds of men, whose knowledge ought to have made them wiser. I am ready, indeed, to grant that the study of the Greek and Latin languages ought not to be enjoined on every youth who seeks to gain, in any degree, a literary and scientific education. If a young man should contemplate being a merchant, or an artist, or extensive planter, or a mechanic, I should by no means urge him to devote much of his time to the study of classic literature. Yet if even such an one had leisure for it, and could afford the expense, he might be better qualified to adorn and to enjoy the pursuit to which he devoted himself, by the richest classical acquirements. Not only might he derive from that species of knowledge a rational and very elevated enjoyment, by the gratification of taste, but he might be able to conduct his employment, whatever it was, upon a more liberal scale, upon more improved principles, and with a taste and intelligence wholly unattainable without it. I would certainly say, then, to every young man who could command the means for the purpose, "Whatever may be your contemplated pursuit in life, make a point of gaining as much classic literature as you can. It will be an ornament and a gratification to you as long as you live. It will enlarge your views, discipline your mind, augment your moral and intellectual power, and prepare you for more extensive and elevated usefulness."

Such would be my address to every young man who had the opportunity of making the attainment in question. But with respect to what is denominated a "liberal education," such an education as is commonly understood to be given in colleges, all intelligent men, all except a few intellectual fanatics, contend for classical literature as an indispensable part of the course. May it ever continue to be so! When colleges cease to make the study of Greek and Latin a necessary and a prominent part of their plan of instruction, I hope they will abandon their charters, and no longer perpetrate the mockery of conferring degrees.

It is no longer, then, an open question, whether you shall devote some measure of your attention to the study of the Greek and Latin languages. You must be in some degree acquainted with this branch of knowledge, if you would gain the honours of the College of New Jersey. But I wish you, my dear sons, to go much further than this. It is my earnest desire and injunction, that you make the ancient languages an object of special attention; that in whatever else you are deficient, you make it a point to be strong and thorough-going here. My reasons for this injunction are the following:

A knowledge of the laws of language, and of the

right use of speech, may be said to be a radical matter, both in gaining and imparting all other kinds of knowledge. He who would express, on any subject, exactly what he means, and be able to know exactly what others mean, must have an exact acquaintance with the principles and powers of language. The study of the laws of written and vocal speech, therefore, must lie at the foundation of all intellectual teaching and attainment. This will be disputed by no one who is qualified to judge in the case.

Now it is impossible for any one to understand the essential principles of grammar, without being acquainted with more languages than one. All scholars are unanimous in maintaining this position. But if we must learn more languages than one, in order to comprehend the general laws which govern human speech, it is surely desirable to become acquainted with the most perfect languages with which the world has ever been favoured. In regard to those languages which have the highest claim to this character, there is great unanimity of opinion among learned men. All agree that among the languages within our reach the Greek and Latin are the most perfect instruments, for the expression of human thought, that the world has ever known. They are more precise and copious in their idioms; more rich and expressive in their vocabulary; more happy in their collocation; and more delicately clear, transparent and comprehensive in their whole structure than any other languages with which we are acquainted. "It is the appropriate praise of the best writers in those languages, that they present us with examples of the most exquisite beauty of thought and expression, united with inimitable simplicity; that they scarcely ever present us with one idle or excrescent phrase or word; that they convey their meaning with a brevity, a directness, a clearness, and a force, which have never been exceeded. Their lines dwell upon our memory. Their sentences have the force of oracular maxims. Every part is vigorous, and very seldom can anything be changed but for the worse. We wander in a scene where everything is luxuriant, yet everything vivid, graceful and correct." Surely, then, those who wish to become acquainted with the power of language as an instrument of thought; with the most delicate and discriminating shades of meaning which it is capable of expressing; with those happy turns of expression by which every thought may be conveyed in the most clear, direct and forcible manner, can engage in no study better adapted to refine, enrich, and enlarge the mind, than that of those noble dialects, which served for so many ages as instruments of instruction and eloquence to the great master minds of the ancient world. Surely he who undervalues and neglects these languages, is chargeable with undervaluing and neglecting some of the noblest objects and means of knowledge that can well engage the attention of the student of literature or science.

It is also worthy of serious consideration that Greek is the original language of part of the Holy Scriptures; and that a deep acquaintance with classical Greek is a most important accomplishment in one who undertakes to be a skilful interpreter of the inspired volume. This consideration will not fail to be appreciated by every enlightened scholar, and especially by all who have in view the sacred office.

Another important consideration here is often not duly regarded. In the Greek and Latin languages there are hidden from the vulgar eye treasures of knowledge, which are richly worthy of being explored, but which can never be fully laid open, excepting to those who understand those languages. Ancient Greece and Rome furnish us with the finest models of history, of poetry, and of various objects of science and taste, which the world has ever possessed. To be ignorant of these models, and of all the facts and principles of which they form the dress and the vehicle, is indeed to deprive ourselves of an amount of knowledge of which it is difficult adequately to estimate the value. Let none say, that the noblest monuments of Grecian and Roman genius may be fully made known to us by translation. No competent judge of the matter ever imagined that this was possible. No ancient classic was ever so translated as to give an adequate idea of the original. The facts which they state may, indeed, be exhibited in a modern tongue; but their native exquisite beauties can never be expressed in such a manner as to be fully comprehended in another language. They must ever continue to be a hidden treasure to all, but those who can hold communion with the language of the original writer. Aside, however, from the necessary imperfection of all translations from the Greek and Latin tongues, let it be remembered, that large stores of knowledge, embodied in those languages, have never been translated at all into English; and, of course, are entirely beyond the reach of the mere English reader.

Besides, let it not be forgotten, that some of the ablest productions of the seventeenth century, that age of genius and of profound erudition, were written in the Latin language. The most valuable treatises of Bacon, Newton, and other master spirits of that age, first appeared in Latin. But is it not humiliating to one, claiming to be a scholar, to be unable to commune with those eminent authors in their original dress?

But more than this; we cannot really understand our own vernacular tongue without a knowledge of Greek and Latin. No one can take the slightest survey of the English language, or of any of the modern languages of Europe, without observing how largely all of them are made up of derivatives from Greek and Latin. We can scarcely utter a sentence, especially in any of the higher walks of discourse, without using many terms, the exact meaning of which cannot be adequately understood without a knowledge of the tongues from which they are derived. We may, indeed, without this knowledge, have some general idea of the meaning of the terms thus employed, but of their precise meaning and force we cannot be adequate judges without knowing something of their etymology. And hence, though we sometimes find those who never learned Greek or Latin, who speak and write their own language with force, and sometimes even with eloquence; yet, even in such speakers and writers, the real scholar may generally discern the absence of that precision, appropriateness and felicity of expression which can only be attained by familiarity with the ancient classics.

Nor is even this all. When we turn to the technical language of any one art or science in popular use—the language, for example, of Chemistry, of Zoology, of Botany, of Mineralogy, of Geology, &c., we shall find it almost all borrowed from the Greek or Latin; and, of course, the students of these sciences, though they may, with great labour, learn the meaning of these terms by rote; yet how much better to begin the study with such a knowledge of the ancient classics as will save the toil of committing to memory the import of terms which, to the ear of the scholar, would proclaim their meaning as soon as pronounced. It is evident, therefore, that he who addresses himself to the study of any of the branches of knowledge of which I speak, having previously acquired a competent knowledge of Greek and Latin, will find his labour more than half abridged, and will proceed with more ease, with more intelligence, and with more accuracy at every step.

If, then, you desire to obtain a clear knowledge and thorough mastery of language as an instrument of thought; if you desire to be really at home in your own language; if you wish to form a pure, precise, lucid, happy style; if you would furnish yourselves with a happy instrumentality for entering and advantageously pursuing every other branch of knowledge; if you would become master, either in speaking or writing, of a rich, copious, exact, discriminating vocabulary; if you would gain that knowledge of antiquity which will serve an invaluable purpose whatever your pursuits may be, and which in some professions is indispensable; if you would adopt one of the most effectual means for the discipline of the mind; if you desire to be able to read the best English classics with the highest degree of taste, pleasure, and profit; and if you would be furnished with some of the very finest means of ornament and illustration in all the higher walks of discourse—make a point of being, as far as possible, profound and accurate classical scholars. Rich attainments in this department of knowledge will shed a lustre and a glory over every other. They will render the study of every other more easy, more pleasant, and more valuable. They will enlarge your minds, and your power of applying them both usefully and ornamentally, to an extent not easily measured. And if, in the providence of God, you should fail of success in any particular profession, a thorough knowledge of the classics will open a door to emolument and honour, in whatever part of the world, or in whatever circumstances you may be thrown. Were I called upon to mention that accomplishment which, united with a fair moral and religious character, would most certainly secure to its possessor an ample and respectable support, I should undoubtedly say, it is that of a sound and accurate classical scholar.

Let me enjoin it upon you, then, in every part of your college course to pay special and unremitting attention to the Greek and Latin classics. Study some portion of them every day, whether your prescribed task requires it or not. Never pass over a sentence without analysing it thoroughly, and going to the bottom both of its terms and its connected import. Never let a week pass without engaging in both Greek and Latin composition. Familiarize yourselves to double translations, i. e. *from* these languages, and *into* them again. I hardly know a more rigorous and improving intellectual discipline than that of faithful and accurate translations from the ancient classics, and then, laying the book aside, attempting to restore the original. Be in the habit of committing to memory passages of remarkable significance and beauty in those languages; and think it not too much to form a little club of half a dozen fellow students for the purpose of speaking Latin, whenever you come together. If I had my collegial life to live over again, I would certainly make a point of forming such an association, and of being one of its members. Its members should spend an hour together at least once a week; and one of its strictest rules should be not to utter a single word in conversation, when together, in any other language than Greek or Latin. This is a hint, rely upon it, worthy of regard. I have repeatedly been placed in circumstances in which I had no means of conversing with learned foreigners but in Latin. To be able to speak it with some degree of readiness, is not only a great convenience, but an elegant accomplishment.

But while, among the regular studies of the college, I unhesitatingly assign the first place in importance to classic literature, I must, with equal decision, assign the second place to mathematics, as one of those radical, governing studies which diffuse over the whole mind, and all its acquirements, a salutary influence.

It is a common thing for young men to dislike mathematics, and to consider a taste for this department of knowledge, as the mark of a plodding and dull mind. They conceive of its principles as insufferably dry, and of its results as in a great measure useless. Hence they are often known to despise it, and to boast of their having no taste for it. But can it be that the science of numbers and quantity; the science which treats so essentially of the relations and proportions of things; the science which investigates and establishes truth by the closest possible reasoning, nay, by the most rigid demonstration, can be a study of small value, or of doubtful benefit? Can it be that such a science, either in respect to its intrinsic character, or its influence on the minds of those who study it, can be of little use? None but the grossly igno-

rant can entertain such an opinion. The fact is, as the study of language lies at the foundation of all accurate acquirement, and all successful communication of knowledge; so the essential principles of mathematics, in the widest sense of that term, may be said to enter more deeply into all the processes of analysis and demonstrative reasoning, than can be stated in a short compass. The influence of this branch of study on the intellectual powers, is connected with the most salutary discipline. It prepares and accustoms the mind to examine the relations of things; to deduce and weigh evidence; to pursue close and rigid reasoning; and to guard against the errors of false deduction. Though you may never have much occasion in your future lives to make any direct use of the algebra or the geometry which you may acquire in college; though you may never be called upon to survey a piece of land, to conduct a ship on the ocean, to calculate a parallax, or an eclipse, or to estimate the height of a mountain, or the distance of a planet; though you may sometimes imagine, when you are required to repeat the demonstrations of Euclid, and to enter into the niceties of Integral and Differential Calculus, that they will never be of any use to you in time to come;—yet, be assured, there never was a greater mistake. No young man can pursue studies better adapted to enlarge and discipline his mind; to subject it to legitimate rule; to form the best reasoning habits; to prepare him for analysing the most abstruse subjects, and for tracing and collecting the most complicated and diverging rays of evidence. In short, if I were perfectly sure that my sons would never have occasion while they lived, to make any immediate practical use of a single mathematical study to which they devoted their time, I would still say, by all means study these subjects with persevering diligence and ardour. They will benefit your minds, and facilitate the acquisition of other branches of knowledge in a thousand ways, of which you can now very imperfectly conceive.

The mineralogist, the geologist, the chemist, and the professor of the healing art, often need to call mathematical science to their aid, as well as the surveyor, the navigator, and the practical astronomer. The advocate at the bar, in a multitude of cases, cannot do even tolerable justice, either to his cause, or his client, without an acquaintance with the principles of mathematics. And scarcely any department of natural philosophy can be advantageously studied, and some of them not at all, without the aid of this noble science. Accordingly, the author of "Lacon, or many things in few words," remarks, "He that gives a portion of his time and talent to the investigation of mathematical truth, will come to all other questions with a decided advantage over his opponents. He will be in argument what the ancient Romans were in the field. To them the day of battle was a day of comparative recreation; because they were ever accustomed to exercise with arms much heavier than those with which they fought; and their reviews differed from a real battle in two respects; they encountered more fatigue, but the victory was bloodless."

The young man, then, who in the course of his education neglects or undervalues mathematics, betrays an ignorance and a narrowness of views of the most ignoble kind. He congratulates himself, perhaps, on a conquest over his teachers, and on a happy escape from the demands of an unwelcome task. But he cheats and injures himself a thousand fold more than his teachers. He incurs a loss and a disadvantage which he can never repair. He foregoes a mental discipline, and a species of mental furniture, for the want of which nothing can adequately compensate. Rely upon it, the more radical and complete your mathematical attainments, the better fitted you will be for whatever profession you may choose; the greater will be your power to adorn, and to turn to the best account any profession; the more ample will be your capacity to serve either the church or the world in your generation.

I return, then, to the maxim with which I began. Aim, as far as possible, to stand at the head of your fellow students in every study. Neglect none: slight none. It is impossible to decide concerning any one of them, that it will not be of essential use to you in after life. But if you are emulous to excel in any particular branches, let them by all means be those which I have specified. You may be incredulous now of the entire truth of what has been advanced; but by and by you will see and acknowledge it all. Let me warn you against postponing to admit and realize this until it be too late. For if you fail of making the acquirements in question before the close of your course in college, you will, in all probability, never make them at all.

In enumerating the particular studies which ought to engage the special regard of every young man who wishes to make the most of himself, I would mention, with peculiar emphasis, the art of composition in his own language. I know of no accomplishment more adapted to increase the power of an educated man. Many an individual who has been cut off by disease from the active duties of a public profession, has been enabled to serve his country and the Church of God more extensively and effectually by his pen, than he could have otherwise done in the enjoyment of his best vigour; and many others, who were active and illustrious in their professional character, have rendered themselves still more illustrious and more permanently useful, by their force and eloquence as writers. Would any wise man grudge the intellectual labour which should enable him to write the English language as it has been written by the author of Junius; by Edmund Burke; by Robert Hall; by Thomas Chalmers; by Thomas Babington Macaulay, of Great Britain; to say nothing of a few eminent men in our own country? True, in the writings of these men there is great diversity, and each has beauties and faults peculiar to himself; but in all there is a wonderful power well worthy of emulation.

I have spoken of the labour of learning to write in the masterly manner attained by the eminent men just mentioned, and by others of the last and present century, whose names deserve a place in the same honourable list. And truly, I know of no art in which unwearied, persevering labour is more indispensable to the attainment of high excellence, than that of which I am speaking. It has long been an accredited proverb—*Poeta nascitur, non fit.* But there is hardly an accomplishment to which the principle of this proverb is less applicable than the art of composition. There is no doubt that some acquire it much more easily and readily than others; but in all it requires a degree of study and of practice to which very few are willing to submit. It requires such a careful perusal of the best writers, such a laborious comparison of different styles, such a persevering study of the principles of language, and such an indefatigable repetition of efforts, as no toil can discourage. No one ever wrote well, who did not write much. I care not how great his talents, if he imagines that this kind of excellence will come, so to speak, "in the natural way," and disdains the employment of unwearied labour to attain it, he will pretty certainly fail of success.

The instruction of experience on this subject is ample, and very decisive. To illustrate my position, I might adduce many signal examples. The late Charles James Fox, of Great Britain, as a parliamentary debater, was, perhaps, never exceeded. It is probable that no man ever rose in the English House of Commons who displayed so much eloquence of the true Demosthenian stamp as that celebrated statesman. As a public speaker, he was simple, clear, inexhaustibly rich, profound, and transcendently forcible. But when he took pen in hand, he fell far below himself. All his published works (except his speeches, which were taken from his lips by stenographers) manifest a second or third rate writer. Of the same thing there was quite as signal, though not so celebrated, an example in one of the Southern States, nearly seventy years ago. A gentleman who had consummate powers as a public speaker, who greatly exceeded all his fellow members of the legislative body to which he belonged in bold, fervid and overpowering eloquence, was at the same time, with his pen, powerless. He could scarcely write a common letter without manifesting an awkwardness, a feebleness, and a want of acquaintance with the most obvious rules of grammar, truly discreditable.

Let me entreat you, then, from the very commencement of your course in college, to be liberal and constant in the use of the pen. Let no day pass without writing something. Summon to your aid in this matter all sorts of composition. Write letters, speeches, abstracts of striking, eloquent volumes, which admit of the process; peruse, and re-peruse the best models; and spare no pains to acquire the happy art of embodying and presenting your thoughts in that clear, simple, direct, lively and powerful manner which will indicate that you are familiar with the precepts of the elegant Horace, and with the example of the great Grecian orator.

LETTER XIII.

GENERAL READING.

"Nihil legebat quod non excerperet."—*Plin. Epist.*

"Ex animi relaxatione divitias contrahere."—*Anon.*

My Dear Sons—I take for granted that your reading will not be confined to your class-books. If you possess any measure of that love of knowledge, and of that activity and enlargement of mind which every member of a college must be expected, as a matter of course, to desire and aim at, you will endeavour to carry along with you, through all your college exercises, some portion of what is called general reading;—that is, a kind and an amount of reading which may contribute toward rendering you, not a mere academical student, but a liberal and general scholar.

I also hope that you will see the importance of subjecting this course of general reading to some digested plan, to a sound and discreet system of rules. Surely one who wishes to make the most of the powers that God has given him, and to reach the highest attainments in knowledge, reputation and usefulness, ought not to surrender himself in this matter, or in anything else, to the government of caprice, or of temporary and spasmodic feeling. Nothing is likely to be well done which is not conducted on a plan. I hope, therefore, my dear sons, you will listen to some counsels which I have to give you on this subject. They may not in all respects accord with your taste or your wishes; but they are the result of some experience, and they are offered with the sincerest desire to promote your highest honour and happiness.

I take for granted, indeed, that the studies prescribed by your instructors will be attended to first of all, and will never be neglected. These have the first claim on your time and attention, and cannot, without serious delinquency, be postponed to any incidental or capricious pursuit. We are accustomed to adopt as a maxim, that a man ought to be just before he is generous. So, in the case before us—he who suffers himself to be drawn away to excursive and miscellaneous objects of attention, while the studies of his class are neglected, may give himself credit for liberality and enlargement of mind; but he is guilty of a fraud on himself, as well as on his instructors, and will find in the end, that here, as well as everywhere else, "honesty is the best policy." But I hope your attention to the studies of your class will be so prompt, so zealous, and so seasonably completed, as to allow you some portion of time every day for the reading of which I speak.

Let your general reading, then, be such as is adapted to be useful. Think of the great ends of education. They are to form proper intellectual and moral habits, and to fill the mind with solid, laudable knowledge. And as life is so short, and the field of knowledge so very extensive, we cannot, of course, know everything; we cannot find time to read all the books which are worthy of being read. Of the many within our reach we must make a selection; and that this selection ought to be made with discrimination and judgment, needs no formal proof. The studies prescribed by authority for your classes will occupy, I trust, with indefatigable diligence, the greater part of your time. Need I employ argument to convince you that the reading destined to occupy the interstitial spaces of your time not filled with prescribed studies, should be of a kind adapted to unbend, and, at the same time, to enlighten, to enlarge and invigorate the mind, and to add to the amount of its valuable furniture?

And here, I trust, it is unnecessary to put you on your guard against all that reading which is adapted to corrupt the principles and the heart. Were I to hear that, under the guise of enlarged and liberal reading, you were, in your leisure moments, poring over the pages of Voltaire, Helvetius, and other similar writers, I should consider you as under an awful delusion, and be ready to weep over you, as probably lost to virtue and happiness, to say nothing of piety. The writers to whom I have referred were vile men, who devoted their learning and talents to the worst purposes; who lived in misery, and died in despair themselves; and whose lives and works were adapted to corrupt and destroy all who held intercourse with them. Say not, that he who is forming his opinions, ought to be willing to examine such writers, and see what they have to say for themselves. I should just as soon regard with patience him who should tell me, that I ought to examine and re-examine whether theft, lying, adultery, and murder were really wrong, and whether it was not a mere prejudice to regard them as crimes. No, my sons, be assured such writers can do you nothing but harm. Their impiety and 'complicated corruption may make you despise your species, doubt of everything, hate your duty, and turn away from all the sober principles of action and of enjoyment; but, believe me, they will never make you wiser or happier men. Their speculations may be compared to the operation of poison received into the animal system, which, as long as it is lodged there, can never fail to excite morbid action, but which can seldom or never be wholly expelled. Whatever may be the effect of your reading such books, the result cannot but be unhappy. If you adopt the errors which they contain, they will be your destruction for time and eternity; for they will destroy all sober principle, and all fitness to be useful in life. And even if your moral constitution should be enabled to resist and overcome the poison, it will leave many an ache and pain, and lay the foundation of many a morbid feeling as long as you live.

You ought, then, to be as choice of your books, for what is called general reading, as the prudent man, who is in delicate health, feels bound to be in the selection of his articles of aliment. There is a wide range of reading, comprehending what may properly be called English classics, with which every educated man is expected to have some acquaintance. None of the works belonging to this catalogue are class-books, in the technical sense of that phrase. Of course they are not included in your prescribed studies; and unless you gain some knowledge of them by extra reading, you must leave college without being acquainted with them. This would be at once a disreputable deficiency, and a serious impediment in the way of your making the most of your college course. Surely before you leave college you ought to be able to write in your own language with elegance and force; but how are you to acquire this power without a familiar acquaintance with some of the best writers of that language?

To the list of authors of whom I thus speak, belong Bacon, Shakspeare and Milton, of the seventeenth century, and Addison, Steele, Pope, Thomson, Young, Goldsmith, Johnson, Cowper, Beattie, and a number of others, of the eighteenth; to which may be added Clarendon, Robertson, Hume, and several more who have figured as votaries of the historic muse. In this catalogue I have forborne to insert the names of some writers greatly distinguished as theologians, because, however worthy of universal study, popular feeling does not generally require that they should be the objects of youthful study. But there are two works, even of this class, which I cannot help singling out as indispensable objects of attention on the part of all cultivated thinkers. I refer to Butler's Analogy, and Edwards's treatise on the Will. What would be thought of an educated young man, who had no acquaintance with any of the eminent writers just named, but by hearsay? True, indeed, a few of these writers are not wholly unexceptionable in regard to the moral character of some of their pages; but their intellectual and literary eminence is transcendent; and when read with discrimination and caution, the youthful aspirant to knowledge and eloquence may derive from them the richest advantages. The truth is, without an acquaintance with the mass of these writers, you cannot appreciate the riches, the beauties, or the purity of your vernacular tongue, or hope successfully to train yourselves to a good style of writing. In these writers, too, you will find a great store-house of fine sentiment, as well as of happy diction, adapted greatly to enlarge and elevate the mind, to impart to it the highest polish, and to prepare it for its best efforts. No matter what the profession may be to which you intend to devote your lives. In any and every walk of life you will find a familiarity with these English classics of inestimable value. No man ever heard Alexander Hamilton, or Daniel Webster plead at the bar, without perceiving the potency of the weapons which they continually derived from their acquaintance with this class of writings. Who ever listened to the speeches of John Quincy Adams, or Henry Clay, or any of their noble compeers, in the Senate-house, without recognizing how largely this department of reading added to the riches, the fascination, and the power of their eloquence? It might be supposed, at first view, that the masters of the healing art could derive but little aid, either in practising or teaching their favourite science, from an intimate acquaintance with the best English classics. But the slightest acquaintance with the most distinguished medical writers and teachers of Great Britain, will show the egregious error of this estimate. And who ever attended the lectures, or perused the writings of Dr. Rush, of our own country, not to mention others still living, without perceiving what grace and power this kind of knowledge imparted to all the products of his lips and his pen? With respect to the pulpit, I will not insult your understandings by attempting to show that the large and general reading of which I speak, is of inestimable value in its bearing on the matter, as well as the manner of the instructions given from week to week, by those who occupy the sacred desk. In short, he who expects to be able to address his fellow men, in any situation, or on any subject, in an attractive and deeply impressive manner, without the diligent study of the principles and powers of the language in which he speaks or writes, cherishes a vain expectation. And he who imagines that these principles and powers are to be learned, without the careful study of those writers who have furnished the best examples of both, might as well hope to "gather grapes of thorns, or figs of thistles."

If you are wise, then, you will devote all those hours which you can spare from your prescribed studies to books which you can turn to rich account in disciplining and enlarging your minds, and in filling them with solid furniture. Something, indeed, in making your selection, is to be referred to personal taste; for that reading which is not pursued *con amore*, as well as with close attention, will profit you little; but still judgment ought to be permitted to step in and regulate the taste. He who refuses to do this, and consults his inclination, for the time being alone, will, no doubt, live and die a very small and probably useless man.

In prescribing a plan for general reading for students in college, there is one question which I presume you will not fail to ask, and which I wish to anticipate and answer in this little system of counsels. The question is, whether novels ought to have any place in the list of books assigned for the "general reading" of students. This is a question of exceedingly great importance. When I was myself a student in a college, more than half a century ago, it was far less interesting and momentous as a practical matter than it has now become. At that time the number of this class of writings was so small, and their popular circulation, comparatively, so inconsiderable, that their influence was scarcely worthy of notice compared with that which they now exert, and which they are every day extending. What amount of prevalence and of influence they are to reach at last, is one of those painful portents on which I dare not allow my mind to dwell. In the meantime, with all the solicitude of a father's heart, I will offer you some counsels which, "whether you will hear or whether you will forbear," appear to me worthy of your most serious regard.

That the form of fictitious history to which the name of novel* is given, is not necessarily and in its own nature criminal, will probably be acknowledged by all. Nay, that it may, when constructed on proper principles, and executed in a proper manner, be made productive of solid utility, is too plain to be doubted. It was on this principle that the infinitely wise Author of our holy religion frequently adopted the form of parable for communicating the most important truths to his hearers. And on the same principle, some of the wisest human teachers have used the vehicle of lively and

* Many do not seem to make the proper distinction between the terms Romance and Novel. Yet there is a distinction between them which ought to be kept up. Romance seems properly applicable only to a narrative of extraordinary adventures, not merely fictitious, but wild, extravagant, improbable, far removed from common life, if not bordering on the supernatural; while the word Novel, more strictly, and by exact speakers and writers, is intended to express that species of fictitious writing which professes to instruct or entertain by describing common life and real characters. The earliest fictitious narratives were chiefly of the former kind. They abounded in stories of giants, dragons, enchanted castles, fairies, ghosts, and all the heroic absurdities of knight-errantry. The aim of those who have figured most in the more recent class of fictitious narrative called novels, has been to describe the natural and probable exhibitions of real life, and of modern manners, and to instruct by the ordinary scenes of social and domestic intercourse.

interesting fiction, known to be such at the time, for insinuating into the mind moral and religious lessons, which, in a different form, might not so readily have gained admittance. It is obvious, then, that to this kind of writing, as such, there can be no solid objection. Novels might be so written as to promote the cause of knowledge, virtue, and piety; to lead the mind insensibly from what is sordid and mean, to more worthy pursuits, and to inspire it with elevated and worthy sentiments. Nay, it may be conceded that out of the myriads of novels with which the literary world has been deluged, a few are, in fact, in some degree entitled to this character, and adapted to produce these effects.

But the great unhappiness of modern times in regard to this subject is two-fold; first, in multiplying works of this kind until they bear an inordinate and injurious proportion in the current literature of the day; and, secondly, in constructing many of them upon a plan adapted to degrade virtue and piety, and even to recommend vice, and, of course, to prove seductive and immoral in their whole influence.

Even when such works are perfectly unexceptionable in their moral character; when they are wholly free from anything corrupt, either in language or sentiment, they may be productive of incalculable mischief, if, as now, they are issued in excessive numbers and quantity. Leaving the character of modern novels entirely out of the question, the enormous number of them, which for the last half century has been every day increasing, has become a grievous intellectual and moral nuisance. As long as they were few in number, and were regarded, not as the substance, but only as the seasoning of the literary feast, they occupied but a small portion of public attention. The chief time and attention of the reading portion of the community were mainly devoted to works of substantial value, fitted to strengthen, enlarge, and enrich the mind. But within the last thirty or forty years, the number of works of this class has multiplied so rapidly; they have become so prominent and alluring a part of the current literature of the day; and by their stimulating and inexhaustible variety, have so drawn away the minds of the aged as well as the young from solid works, that they have come to form the principal reading of a large portion of the community, and, of course, have become a snare and an injury to an extent not easily calculated. As long as exhilarating gases, or other stimulating substances, are administered sparingly, and as medicines, they may be altogether harmless, and even essentially useful. But when those who have taken them for some time in this manner become so enamoured with them as to be no longer satisfied with their moderate and salutary use, but make them their daily and principal aliment, they become inevitably mischievous. They destroy the tone of the stomach, and, in the end, radically undermine the health.

So it is with the insidious excitement of novels. Were a young man to take none of them into his hands, but those which might be safely pronounced pure and innocent; and were he certain that he would never be tempted to go beyond the most moderate bounds in seeking and perusing even such, there would, perhaps, be little danger to be apprehended. But no one can be thus certain of either. The general stimulus of fictitious narrative, as actually administered, is morbid and mischievous. It excites the mind, but cannot fill or nourish it. The probability is, that he who allows himself to enter this course, will be led on, like the miserable tippler, from one stage of indulgence to another, until his appetite is perverted; his power of self-denial and self-government lost; and his ruin finally sealed; or, at least, his mind so completely indisposed and unfitted for the sober realities of practical wisdom, for the pursuits of solid science and literature, as to be consigned to the class of superficial drivellers as long as he lives.

The truth is, novels—even the purest and best of

them—with very few exceptions, are adapted, not to instruct, but only to amuse; not to enrich or strengthen the mind, but only to exhilarate it. They bear very much the same relation to genuine mental aliment, that the alcoholic dram does to solid food. They ever enervate the mind. They generate a sickliness of fancy, and render the ordinary affairs and duties of life altogether uninteresting and insipid. After wading through hundreds of the most decent and popular volumes belonging to this class—what has been gained? After consuming so many months of precious time—time which can never be recalled—in this reading, what has been acquired? what has been laid up for future use? Nothing—absolutely nothing! Not a trace of anything really useful has been left behind. The days and nights devoted to their perusal have been lost—totally lost. What infatuation is it for a rational creature, who is sent into the world for serious and important purposes, and who is hastening to a solemn account, thus to waste precious time; and, what is worse, thus to pervert his mind, and, in a greater or less degree, to disqualify himself for sober employments! The celebrated Dr. Goldsmith, in writing to his brother, respecting the education of his son, expresses himself in the following strong terms, which are the more remarkable as he himself had written one of the most popular novels:—"Above all things, never let your son touch a romance or novel. These paint beauty in colours more charming than nature, and describe happiness that man never tastes. How delusive, how destructive are those pictures of consummate bliss! They teach the youthful mind to sigh after beauty and happiness which never existed; to despise the little good which fortune has mixed in our cup, by expecting more than she ever gave; and, in general, take the word of a man who has seen the world, and has studied human nature more by experience than precepts—take my word for it, I say, that such books teach us very little of the world." He might have gone further and said, they teach us little of anything worth knowing, and so pervert the taste as to take away all relish for applying the mind to anything sober or useful. Often have I known young men so bewitched by novels that they could read nothing else. They sought for new works of this class in every direction; devoured them with insatiable avidity; lost all relish for their regular prescribed studies; neglected those studies more and more; and at length closed their college course miserable scholars, and utterly unqualified for any sober pursuit.

But there is another source of evil in this department of literature, still more serious and formidable. A very large proportion of modern novels are far from being innocent. They are positively seductive and corrupting in their tendency. They make virtue to appear contemptible, and vice attractive, honourable, and triumphant. Folly and crime have palliative and even commendatory names bestowed upon them. The omnipotence of love over all obligations and all duties, is continually maintained, and the extravagance of sinful passion represented as the effect of amiable sensibility. That some ladies, and even titled ladies, have appeared in the lists of authorship of such works, is one of the mournful indications of the taste of the present day, and no unequivocal testimony of the danger of this class of writings. And though works of this character may be, at first, contemplated with abhorrence, no one can tell how soon the mind may be gradually and insidiously reconciled to them, by familiarity with their pestiferous and infectious sentiments.

There, is, indeed, a portion of modern novels, which millions of the young and the old have read with eager delight, and pronounced not only innocent but useful; adapted to enlarge our knowledge of human nature, and to inspire generous and benevolent sentiments. These are the numerous works of this class by Sir Walter Scott, and the later and less celebrated, but highly popular works of Mr. Dickens, of South Britain.

With regard to the former, I am constrained to say, that my estimate is less favourable than that of many who admire and praise them. Of the great talents of Sir Walter Scott, as evinced in these and other writings, no competent judge can entertain a doubt; and that his novels abound in elevated sentiments, in graphic delineation, and in powerful diction, from which the aspirant to high literary and moral excellence may learn much, is equally evident. But those who read intelligently such of his works as profess to take a retrospect of Scottish history, interwoven with fiction, if capable of making a proper estimate of the times and characters which he undertakes to portray, will perceive that the writer arrays himself against the patriotism and the piety of some of the best men that ever adorned the history of his country; that he exhibits orthodoxy and zeal under the guise of enthusiasm and fanaticism; that he strives to cover with dishonour "men of whom the world was not worthy," and to elevate and canonize their persecutors; in short, that the general influence of his works is wholly unfriendly to religion. These characteristics pervade some of the most popular of his novels. Ought I, can I, consistently with the most sacred obligations, advise that such books be put into the hands of inexperienced and unsuspecting youth, unaware of danger, and at an age, and in circumstances, most likely to receive serious injury?

The later and highly popular novels of Mr. Dickens, are not liable to the most serious of these objections. They abound in just, and sometimes in striking sentiments, strongly and happily expressed; and they lay open pictures of real life, chiefly of the most sordid, vulgar and vile character, well adapted to impart to youthful readers a knowledge of the world, and especially of the selfish, fraudulent, and degraded world. This is the most favourable side of the portrait. The most serious objections are, that they render the youthful mind familiar with the ingenuity and the arts of low and vulgar crime; that they introduce their readers, as it were, behind the scenes in the drama of systematic and revolting wickedness; and while they tend, more than most writings of this class, to absorb the mind, and give it a distaste for solid knowledge, they impart nothing which can be considered as an equivalent for that which is lost.

Estimating novels, then, not as they might be made, but as they are in fact, it may be asserted that there is no species of reading which, habitually and promiscuously pursued, has a more direct tendency to dissipate and weaken the intellectual powers; to discourage the acquisition of valuable knowledge; to fill the mind with vain, unnatural, and delusive ideas; and to deprave the moral taste. It would, perhaps, be difficult to assign any single cause which has contributed so much to produce that lightness and frivolity which so remarkably characterize the literary taste of the nineteenth century, as the unexampled multiplication, and the astonishing popularity of this class of writings.

I have, therefore, no hesitation, my dear sons, in saying, that, if it were practicable, I would wholly exclude novels from your general reading; not because there are none which may be perused with some profit; but because the hope that, out of the polluted and pestiferous mass continually presented to the youthful mind, a tolerably wise choice will generally, or even in many instances, be made, can scarcely be thought a reasonable hope. If, I could hope to succeed, then, in such counsel, I would say, throw away all your novels. If you wish to form a sober, practical, robust intellectual character, throw them all away; banish them from your study. They will never help you in reaching either usefulness or solid fame.

As, however, these fictitious productions are strewed around us in such profusion, and will more or less excite the curiosity of youth, the plan of total exclusion is seldom practicable. In these circumstances it is, perhaps, the wisest course to endeavour to restrain and regulate the curiosity which cannot be wholly repressed, and to exercise the utmost vigilance in making a proper choice for its gratification, and in restricting this gratification within the smallest possible bounds. For it may, with confidence, be pronounced, that no one was ever an extensive, and especially an habitual reader of novels, even supposing them all to be well selected, without suffering both intellectual and moral injury, and, of course, incurring a diminution of happiness.

But the trash which is everywhere spread around the youth of our land, under the name of novels, is not the only form of light reading that is adapted to dissipate the mind, to degrade the taste, and to work intellectual and moral injury in all who yield to the prevalent mania. The time that is devoted by the young men in our literary institutions to the perusal of literary and political journals, of magazines, and the multiplied forms of light periodicals, which everywhere solicit their attention, forms so serious an evil, that every student who values his time, and desires to attain the solid improvement of his talents, ought to be aware of it, and from the outset of his course, to be on his guard against it. The fact is, the number of ephemeral periodicals has become so enormously great, and they every day so importunately solicit the attention of those who have any taste for reading, that they leave little time for studying anything better. Nor is this all. They distract the attention of the student; seduce him from sources of more profound, systematic, and useful information; and are fitted to form pedants and index hunters, rather than men of real erudition. On this account, the reading of literary young men, within the last forty or fifty years, has become far less solid than formerly. Many of the best works of the seventeenth and eighteenth centuries have been crowded out of view by compends, compilations, and a thousand ephemeral productions; not merely because the taste for better works has been in a great measure lost, by superficial habits; but because the number of these ephemeral and catchpenny trifles is so great as absolutely to leave little time, and, in many cases, no time for anything better.

There is no doubt that the seventeenth century was the age of genius. The eighteenth, it is acknowledged, exceeded it in taste; but in original powerful thinkers, the seventeenth appears to me to stand unrivaled. He who will look over the list of the eminent men who, during that century, adorned Great Britain and the continent of Europe, will be, I cannot doubt, of the opinion, that no such catalogue can be found in any other age of the last eighteen hundred years. To say nothing of the illustrious divines who distinguished that period, who can recollect the names of Bacon, Shakspeare, Newton, Selden, Boyle, Hale, Locke, Milton, Coke, Des Cartes, Grotius, Leibnitz, Galileo, the Bernoulis, and many more, without feeling that they were among the mightiest minds that the world ever saw? These men were the great original thinkers of modern times; and certainly those who allow themselves to be ignorant of their works, forego one of the richest means of enlightening and invigorating the mind within their reach. How unwise, then, are those youth, who, while they profess to be students, profess to be seeking the best improvement of their talents, the best preparation to shine in the highest walks of life, really adopt a course adapted to make them superficial triflers, instead of men of solid, profound, and powerful accomplishments! Rely upon it, if you wish to take rank with any of the eminent men whose names have been mentioned as adorning the seventeenth century, or even with many who have appeared in our own country within the last fifty years, you must devote yourselves as they did, to solid, systematic, and unwearied study, and not waste your time with the periodicals and compends which may, from time to time, engage the popular attention.

After writing the above, I was not a little gratified to find my opinion confirmed by so competent an authority as that of Judge Story, of Massachusetts, whose taste, scholarship, and sound judgment impart peculiar weight to his decisions on such a subject, especially when it is recollected that none who know him will ascribe to him that tendency to puritanical rigour, that may be thought by some to be allied to such counsels as have been expressed.

In a late discourse, addressed to the Alumni of his *Alma Mater*, in which he treats of "the dangers, the difficulties, and the duties of scholars in our own age, and especially in our own country," that eminent scholar and jurist delivers the following opinions, which I hope you will seriously consider:

"Who that looks around him does not perceive, what a vast amount of the intellectual power and energy of our own country is expended, not to say exhausted, upon temporary and fugitive topics,—upon occasional addresses—upon light and fantastic compositions—upon manuals of education, and hand-books of instruction,—upon annotations and excerpts,—and upon the busy evanescent discussions of politics, which fret their hour upon the stage, or infest the halls of legislation? Need we be told that honours thus acquired melt away at the very moment when we grasp them; that some new wonder will soon usurp their place; and, in its turn, will be chased away or dissolved by the next bubble or flying meteor? I know that it has sometimes been said, that 'nothing popular can be frivolous; and that what influences multitudes must be of proportionate importance.' A more dangerous fallacy, lurking under the garb of philosophy, could scarcely be stated. There would be far more general truth in the statement of the very reverse proposition. Our lecture-rooms and lyceums are crowded, day after day, and night after night, with those who seek instruction without labour, and demand improvement without effort. We have abundance of zeal, and abundance of curiosity enlisted in the cause, with little aim at solid results, or practical ends. It seems no longer necessary, in the view of many persons, for students to consume their midnight lamps in pale and patient researches,—or in communing with the master spirits of other days,—or in interrogating the history of the past,—or in working out, with a hesitating progress, the problem of human life. An attendance upon a few courses of lectures upon science, or art, or literature, amidst brilliant gas-lights, or brilliant experiments, or brilliant discourses of accomplished rhetoricians, is deemed a satisfactory substitute for hard personal study, in all the general pursuits of life. Nay, the capital stock thus acquired may be again retailed out to less refined audiences, and give ready fame and profit to the second-hand adventurer.

"It is an old saying, that there is no royal road to learning; and it is just as true now as it was two thousand years ago. Knowledge, deep, thorough, accurate, must be sought, and can be found only by strenuous labour, not for months, but for years; not for years, but for a whole life. What lies on the surface is easily seen, and easily measured. What lies below is slowly reached, and must be cautiously examined. The best ore may often require to be sifted and purified. The diamond slowly receives its polish under the hands of the workman, and then only gives out its sparkling lights. The very marble whose massy block is destined to immortalize some great name, reluctantly yields to the chisel; and years must elapse before it becomes (as it were) instinct with life, and stands forth the breathing image of the original.

"It cannot admit of the slightest doubt (at least in my judgment) that the habit of desultory and miscellaneous reading, thus created, has a necessary tendency to enervate the mind, and to destroy all masculine thinking. Works of a solid cast, which require close attention and exact knowledge to grapple with them, are thrown aside, as dull and monotonous. We apologize to ourselves for our neglect of them, that they may be taken up at a more convenient season; or we flatter ourselves that we have sufficiently mastered their contents and merits from the last Review, although, in many cases, it may admit of a doubt, whether the critic himself has ever read the work. Without stopping to inquire, how many of the whole class of literary readers now study with thoughtful diligence, the standard writers in our own language, and are not content with abridgments, or manuals, or extracts, I would put it to those who are engaged in the learned professions, and have the most stringent motives for deep, thorough, and exact knowledge—I would put it to them to say, how many of their whole number devote themselves to the study of the great masters of their profession; how many of them can, in the sober language of truth, say, We are at home in the pages of our profoundest authors; we not only possess them to enrich our libraries, but we devote ourselves to the daily consultation of them. They are beside us at our firesides, and they cheer our evening studies. We live and breathe in the midst of their laborious researches, and systematical learning."*

Such are the sentiments of this eminent man. I know that, in your sober judgment, you cannot but approve them. If so, let it be seen that you begin now, even within the college walls, to waste as little time as possible on the ephemeral trifles of the day, and to employ as much as possible on those rich works of classical character and value, every one of which will add something to your permanent stores of intellectual wealth.

But if you wish to profit much by this counsel, you must have a plan about it. Resolve, then, that you will be a sparing reader of periodicals of every kind. Seldom allow yourselves to employ many minutes over a newspaper, unless it be to peruse a great speech, or some other document of more than common interest. A large part of the reading furnished by our newspa-

* A Discourse delivered before the Society of the Alumni of Harvard University. By Joseph Story, LL. D.

pers is of a highly demoralizing character; and the greater portion of those which belong to the penny class, are most polluting in their tendency. Turn from magazines and novels as you would from a suspicious, not to say, an infected region; touching none of them, or, if any, none but a few of the best, and devoting as little time as possible even to them. Keep constantly at your elbow, in a course of reading, some English classic, adapted at once to cultivate your taste and add to your stock of knowledge; and to be taken up when your prescribed labour is terminated. How much better to have a system of this sort, than to pass the hours of relaxation from the studies of your class, either in perfect idleness and *ennui*, or in reading the most worthless, not to say the vilest trash, that is so often engaging the attention of students who profess to aim at the attainment of liberal knowledge! If the plan I have recommended, or anything like it, were faithfully pursued, every student of college, before the close of his regular course, would be familiar with the best masters of sentiment, of diction, and of knowledge that the English language affords.

But I hope you will not confine your general reading to the English language. That student in college is greatly wanting to himself, who, in the present extended, and greatly extending intercourse among nations, does not labour, as far as possible, to become acquainted with several modern languages, and especially with the French and German. The subserviency of these languages to professional eminence and success is obvious. I have repeatedly known lawyers and physicians who resided in populous places, submit, late in life, to the labour of acquiring both those languages, because they perceived that the possession of them would serve as an introduction to a large portion of lucrative business. How much better would it have been for such persons to have acquired a knowledge of these languages in college; at an age when a new language is more easily gained than in more advanced life, and when the range of its utility would have been far greater! I rejoice to know that you have not been inattentive to the languages specified, and that you are in some measure prepared to avail yourselves of the benefits to which they may be made subservient.

Let a part of your general reading be in those languages; as well for the enlargement of your knowledge, as for the increase of your familiarity with different dialects. In French, read such works as Fenelon's Telemaque; the sermons of Massillon, Bossuet, Bourdaloue, and Saurin; Voltaire's Siècle de Louis XIV. et XV., and Histoire de Charles XII., and his La Henriade, (avoiding the great mass of the other works of that profligate infidel;) together with the works of Chateaubriand, Lamartine, De Tocqueville, Guizot, and Ballanche, of the present day, and especially Professor Merle d'Aubigné's Histoire de la Reformation, a most instructive and graphic work, and to read which in the original, it would be well worth while to acquire the French language.

With regard to German reading, my knowledge is too scanty to enable me to speak in a very adequate or discriminating manner. But I may, without hesitation, recommend that the hours bestowed upon it may be given to the writings of such men as Klopstock, Gellert, Wieland, Herder, Gœthe, Schiller, and a few more, whose character you will readily learn from German scholars. It is to be lamented that the writings of most of these men ought to be read with caution, as by no means wholly faultless in their tendency. Still, in a literary point of view, they may be considered as holding a high place in the country to which they belong, and as among the best that can be recommended to those who wish for a small amount of select German reading.

It will readily be perceived, from all that has been said, that the thing popularly called general reading, is a matter of no small importance; that it affords a noble opportunity for enriching the mind with valuable knowledge; that the variety in this field, which solicits the attention of the scholar, is immense; and, of course, that he who wastes the precious hours, which he can afford to devote to this employment, in the perusal of works frivolous, corrupt, or, to say the least, wholly unprofitable, is equally foolish and criminal. The truth is, a wise youth may render his general reading as essentially subservient to his ultimate success in life, as the most solid prescribed study in which he can engage.

LETTER XIII.

ATTENTION.—DILIGENCE.

"Μελέτη τὸ πᾶν."—*Periander.*

———"Nil sine magno
Vita labore dedit mortalibus."—*Hor.*

My Dear Sons—When man fell from God, a part of the sentence pronounced upon him, in the way of penalty, was—"In the sweat of thy brow thou shalt eat thy bread." It was indeed a penalty; and, of course, all the labour and toil connected with success in life, ought to remind us of our fallen nature, and humble us under the mighty hand of God. But the penalty in this, and in many other cases, has been converted by the wisdom and goodness of God into a blessing. The great law of our being, that we shall eat our bread in the sweat of our brow, extends much further than is commonly imagined. Many understand it as applying only to the common labourer. But it applies to all. All who would enjoy life—all who would have bread to eat in plenty and comfort, must labour for it either in body or mind. And is it not a mercy that the providence of God has so ordered it? What would be the consequence if all could eat and drink, and enjoy the luxuries of life to their heart's content, without labour? Would it not dissolve the bonds of society, and convert the world into a real hell? The law of labour, in one form or another impressed upon all men, tends to promote their health, both of body and mind;

to excite, invigorate and expand their faculties; to preserve them from the rust of inaction, and the snares of idleness; to discipline and elevate both the intellectual and moral character, and to make man a helper and a blessing to man.

You ought to regard it, then, not as a misfortune, but as a blessing, that much knowledge is not to be gained, nor a high reputation established, without much labour. Of course I cannot sympathize with those who lament this arrangement of Providence. Rather ought we all to rejoice in it, as one of the multiplied evidences of that adorable wisdom and benignity, which brings light out of darkness, order out of confusion, and results the most blessed and happy out of circumstances painful to our natural feelings.

I take for granted that my sons, after going so far in the attainment of what is called a liberal education, expect to get their living without mechanical labour. But if they hope to accomplish anything worthy of pursuit, either in the acquisition of knowledge, or in the formation of good intellectual and moral habits, and serving their generation acceptably and usefully, without much labour and toil, they were never more deluded. If one old heathen could say, in the language of the mottoes, which stand at the head of this letter, "In this life nothing is given to mortals, without great labour;" and another, "Industry and care effect everything;" much more strongly and clearly is the same lesson taught by the word of God, and by uniform experience. Think not that what is called genius, or even the highest order of talents, even if you could persuade yourselves that you possessed them, would exempt you from the law of patient labour. The greatest men that ever adorned and benefited human nature, have found it otherwise. The fact is, any single branch, either of literature or science, if we would thoroughly master it, is deep enough and wide enough, to keep indefatigably busy the most vigorous and active mind for a long lifetime. How much more the multiplied branches, which he, who aspires to shine in any one of the learned professions, is compelled to explore! There is, no doubt, great diversity in regard to the ease and readiness with which some minds acquire knowledge compared with others. But in no case whatever can a large amount of knowledge, on any subject, be gained without much patient labour. And it is simply the want of a disposition to submit to this labour which makes so many miserable scholars, and which stands in the way of that success in life which might have been otherwise easily and certainly commanded.

A defect here, my dear sons, lies more frequently and more deeply at the foundation of those failures to get forward in life, which are so frequently seen and lamented, than is commonly imagined. One of the most sagacious and successful managers of secular business that I ever knew, who was, for many years, a faithful and efficient trustee of our college, and to whom she owes a large debt of gratitude for his wise and useful services as one of her guardians,* when any one was spoken of in his presence as failing of success in his temporal affairs, and when the want of success was accounted for by calling him unfortunate, was heard more than once to say—"Unfortunate! don't tell me; when I hear of such an event I set it down to the score of the want of industry, or of discretion, or both. No industrious, prudent man need be in want or in difficulty in this country." This, in general, I believe to be a true verdict. With very few exceptions, (and exceptions there doubtless are,) I am inclined to believe that the opinion of that enlightened judge may be confidently maintained. It will be found true in ninety-nine cases out of an hundred.

If this remark applies with justice to the ordinary details of commercial or mechanical business, it is no less applicable to mental efforts and attainments.

* The late Robert Lenox, Esquire, of New York.

Here you might just as well expect any absurdity, any impossibility to occur, as the gaining of any large amount of digested, valuable knowledge without much and indefatigable mental labour. When I have heard, therefore, as I sometimes have, of students (if they deserve the name of students) who dreamed that they were men of genius, and who imagined that genius, without industry, would accomplish everything—nay, who felt ashamed of appearing studious, and who endeavoured to conceal the little mental application to which they did submit, by conducting it in a stealthy manner;—when I have heard of such young men, I have hardly known which to admire most—their childish ignorance of the nature of true knowledge, or their miserable charlatanry in aping a character to which they had no just claim.

If you wish to be real scholars, and to make any solid attainments in any of the branches of knowledge to which your attention is directed, calculate on constant indefatigable labour. Abhor the thought of skimming over the surface of anything. Whatever labour it may cost, go to the bottom, as far as you possibly can, of every subject. Give yourselves no rest until you comprehend the fundamental principles, the *rationale* of everything. I need not say to any one who thinks, that it is only when a subject is thus studied that our attainments deserve the name of knowledge. Then only can it be said to have a firm lodgment in the mind, and to be ready for practical use when subsequently needed. On the one hand, never give way to the foolish notion, that you can never advantageously study a particular branch without a special genius for it. Many an infatuated youth, for example, has tried to excuse himself for not mastering or loving his mathematical studies, by pleading that he has no genius for that branch of science. Never allow yourselves to offer or to entertain such a plea. A young man of any mind ought to be ashamed of such a thought. It is, in forty-nine cases out of fifty, the offspring of either mental imbecility, or shameful laziness. What though Dean Swift was disgraced in the University of Dublin by his ignorance of mathematics? Does any one doubt that, if morbid caprice and indolence had not stood in the way, he might have been an eminent mathematical scholar? And is not every reflecting reader of his life persuaded that, if he had been such a scholar, he would have been a far greater, and, perhaps, a more practically happy man? No one who has the spirit of a man ought to consider any department of knowledge as beyond his reach. Let him be willing to labour in the attainment of it and he will overcome. Let him constrain himself, however reluctantly, to engage in the study; and, in a little while, that which in the outset was a toil will become a real pleasure.

On the other hand, imagine not that any department of knowledge can be successfully explored and gained without long-continued and patient labour. If, indeed, you wish for a mere smattering, which will enable you to appear decently at a recitation, and plausibly to repeat a lesson by rote, without understanding what you say; then, truly, you may get along without much labour. But what is implied in filling the mind with real digested knowledge? Facts must be stored up; principles must be investigated and mastered; relations, proximate and remote, must be explored; and all applied to the numberless and ever varying cases which the works of nature and of art present. Now, can any thinking mind imagine, that this is to be done without much mental labour; without continued, systematic, unwearied toil from day to day? Dr. Johnson never uttered a juster sentiment than when he said—"Every one who proposes to grow eminent by learning, should carry in his mind, at once, the difficulty of excellence, and the force of industry; and remember that fame is not conferred, but as the recompense of labour; and that labour, vigorously continued, has not often failed of its reward."*

* Rambler, No. 25.

There is, I apprehend, no defect more common among students than impatience of protracted labour in the acquisition of knowledge. Many seem to imagine that large and profound views of the most difficult subjects are to be gained by one or a few mighty efforts; by an occasional spasmodic exertion, if I may so express it. Be assured, whatever may be the case with a rare genius, now and then, it is commonly not so. The old French proverb, "*Pas à pas on va bien loin*," i. e. "Step by step one goes very far," affords the real clew to the proper course. A mountain is not to be passed by a single leap; nor a deep and rich mine to be explored by a single stroke, or even a few strokes, of the spade. But a sufficient number of slow, cautious, patient efforts will accomplish the enterprise. So it is in study. Impatient haste is the bane of intellectual work. A little thoroughly done, every day, will make no contemptible figure at the end of the year. We are told of Sir Isaac Newton, that, when questioned respecting the peculiar powers of his own mind, he said, that if he had any talent which distinguished him from the common mass of thinking men, it was the power of slowly and patiently examining a subject; holding it up before his mind from day to day, until he could look at it in all its relations, and see something of the principles by which it was governed. His estimate was probably a correct one. His most remarkable, and certainly his most valuable, talent consisted, not in daring, towering flights of imagination, or in strong creative powers, but in slow, plodding investigation; in looking at a series of facts, from day to day, until he began to trace their connection; to spell out their consequences; and ultimately to form a system as firm as it was beautiful. The little structures, which haste and parsimony of labour have erected from time to time, have stood their passing day, and soon crumbled into ruins. But the mighty pyramids, built up by long, patient, and unwearied labour, have continued firm, in all their unshaken grandeur, amidst the waste of ages.

When you contemplate the splendid success of some eminent individuals, now or lately on the stage of public life, you are ready to imagine that similar success is beyond your reach, and that to aim at it would be presumptuous. This is a great mistake, and to indulge it is very unwise. It must be admitted, indeed, that the success of all cannot be alike. All, for example, cannot be great orators; excellence in this art depends so much on physical accomplishments; on the voice, the eye, the nervous temperament, &c., that we can by no means assure every one that a high degree of it is within his reach. Yet even here great excellence may often be attained by those whose qualifications appear, at first view, wholly unpromising. The history of Demosthenes is a most striking exemplification of the truth of this remark. Hundreds who are now poor speakers, if they had the industry and the resolution that the illustrious Grecian had—if they would take the unwearied pains that he did to expand and invigorate the chest, to strengthen and discipline the voice, and to fill their minds with appropriate sentiments and happy diction, such as he attained, might well emulate even his eloquence. It is, undoubtedly, mere indolence, or ill directed effort, which stands in the way of high attainment, in this rarest of all human accomplishments.

But the avenues to real greatness are almost infinitely diversified; and if one be shut, another is open to almost every one. I think, my dear sons, that my estimate of your talents is not extravagant. I am willing, for argument's sake, to place it as low as any one can ask; and I will still say, that great things are within your reach. Nay, I will venture confidently to affirm, that every one who has had mind enough and knowledge enough to reach any class in college, has it in his power, humanly speaking, to attain high distinction as a beloved, honoured, and eminently useful man.

Some of the greatest benefactors of society that ever lived were not men of genius; but they were sober and industrious, willing to labour in laying up knowledge; and they did thus lay it up, and having attained it, they had the honesty and the benevolence to employ it all in endeavouring to promote the welfare and happiness of their fellow men. Who can say that this is beyond his reach? Look round on your classmates, and ask, which of them is too low on the score of talent to be thus eminently and honourably useful, if he were only willing to undergo the requisite labour for the purpose? While laziness and vice are every day clouding the prospects and degrading the reputation of thousands, making them cumberers of the ground, instead of benefactors of their species; there is no doubt that, in a multitude of cases, the mere qualities of unwearied industry and inflexible honesty have exalted men of plain talents to the highest ranks of usefulness and honour. Why, O why are so few willing, who have it in their power, to make the experiment?

But there is such a thing as being incessantly occupied, and yet not industrious. This is the case with him who has no regular system of employment, who is constantly the sport of new occurrences; who is continually getting in arrears with his business, and always in a hurry to overtake it, but never able. Such persons never accomplish much, and their work, such as it is, is hardly ever done in time. I once knew a most worthy man, an alumnus of our college, who had an active mind, and who was seldom idle. But he had not the power of pursuing any one object long at a time. He was incessantly forming new projects of literary works, but never carried any one of them into execution. I seldom met him without finding his mind occupied with some new scheme, and having apparently altogether abandoned that which absorbed his attention at the date of the preceding interview. The consequence was, that, although conscientious, pious, and by no means idle, his life was comparatively wasted in promises never realized, and in efforts altogether abortive. Real industry is that which wisely and maturely forms a plan, which firmly and patiently pursues it from day to day, until it is brought to a plenary conclusion. Perseverance is one of the essential qualities of genuine industry. He who works with zeal and diligence for a few days, and then either breaks off altogether, or suffers himself to be interrupted by every frivolous occurrence, will never build up a very firm or elevated fame. "How is it that you accomplish so much?" said a friend to the great pensioner, De Witt, of Holland. "By doing one thing at a time," replied the eminent statesman.

How many hours *per diem* you ought to study, and in what precise way these hours ought to be distributed in the twenty-four, I shall not attempt to prescribe. This depends so much on the state of health, the physical temperament, and the diversified circumstances of each individual, that it is impossible to lay down a rule which shall suit all equally well. Some, who study with intense application whenever they are thus engaged, ought not to employ in this manner more than six hours each day; while those whose application of mind in such cases is less intense and absorbing, may venture on ten or even twelve hours in every twenty-four, without injury. The slow and phlegmatic must, of course, employ more time over their books than those whose mental operations are more rapid and ardent. But see that, as far as possible, no moment be either lost in vacuity or wasted on frivolity.

It is truly wonderful to think how much may be accomplished by order mingled with diligence in our pursuits. He who has a time and a place for everything that he has to do, and who gains, by habit, the power of summoning his powers to the vigorous performance at the proper time, of the prescribed task, will soon learn to accomplish more in a day, than he who is frequently struggling with *ennui* and with indolence will be likely to accomplish in a month.

And if you wish to be successfully industrious, make a point of being early risers. Lying long in bed in the morning is, in every view, a pernicious habit. It seldom fails to exert a morbid influence on the bodily health. It is generally connected with languid feelings, and with want of decision and energy in everything. It may thus be said to cut off a number of years from the ordinary life of man. But the importance of this habit on the employments of a student is incalculable. He who has much to do ought to begin early in the morning, not only because the minds of most people are most active and vigorous immediately after the repose of the night, but also because when a large part of our daily task is early accomplished, the interruptions of company, as the day advances, are less annoying, and less destructive to the progress of our work. Sir Walter Scott, we are told by his biographer, was in the habit, at one period of his life, of having the greater part of his literary task for each day nearly completed at an early hour in the forenoon, thus leaving a number of hours every day to be devoted to the social and other employments, which his eminence and his multiplied connections with his friends and the public unavoidably brought upon him. This too was the great secret of the immense amount of labour accomplished by those eminent men in former times, whose ponderous folios we now look upon with amazement, and can scarcely find time to read. They were early risers. Whenever they had a great task to perform (and they always had some task on hand), they were steady and incessant in their labours. They lost no time in idleness or trifles. Imitate their example, and you may accomplish as much as they did. The laws of the college which call you up at an early hour, and enjoin upon you an early retirement to rest, may now seem to you a hardship; but if you live a few years, you will regard them in a very different light.

LETTER XIV.

ASSOCIATIONS—FRIENDSHIPS.

"*Noscitur a sociis.*"—ANON.

"It is certain that either wise bearing, or ignorant carriage, is caught as men take diseases, one of another; therefore take heed of your company."—SHAKSPEARE.

MY DEAR SONS—I can well remember the time, when, in the prospect of entering a college, my impressions of the character of such an institution were of the most interesting kind. I expected to find myself united to a society of young gentlemen, of polished manners, of honourable feelings and habits, and of ardent and generous literary emulation. I had been experimentally aware that, in inferior seminaries, there are often found lads of vulgar character, and even of profligate principles, and grossly revolting habits. But in a college I expected to find the very *élite* of literary young men; and to meet, in all its classes, and especially in its more advanced ones, circles with whom it would be both delightful and improving to maintain intercourse. Judge, then, of my surprise, when I found that, even in a college, there were sometimes to be seen young men of manners as vulgar and offensive, and of habits and principles as profligate, as elsewhere; nay, in some rare instances, capable of the meanest as well as the most criminal practices; and, therefore, that even here it was necessary to be select in associations, and especially in intimacies. I might have reflected, indeed, that human depravity appears in every connection and walk of life; that he who expects to find it wholly excluded, even from the church of God, cherishes a vain expectation; and that, in circles of college students, it is the part of wisdom to be always on the watch, for ascertaining the character and avoiding the company of those young men whose touch is pollution, and whose intimacy is equally disreputable and perilous.

It is a maxim of inspired wisdom (1 Cor. xv. 33) that "evil communications corrupt good manners." No one, however wise or firm, has a right to consider himself as above the reach of the danger against which we are warned by this maxim. Even the inspired apostle himself, the penman of the maxim, if not protected by a special guardianship, would have been liable to suffer by the mischievous influence against which he guards us. How much greater the danger when the fascination of intercourse with the corrupt is indulged without restraint, and without the least apprehension of mischief?

There are few situations, in which a base and profligate young man is capable of doing more injury to those about him, than in a college. The points of contact between those who study in the same institution, and especially in the same class, are so numerous and important, that it is difficult wholly to avoid contamination. The counsel, therefore, which I have to give on this subject, as it is unspeakably important, so you will find it no less difficult to follow in your daily intercourse.

I take for granted, that you will lay it down as a fundamental principle in your social relations, to treat every fellow student with decorum, and even with urbanity; that you will study to be gentlemen, even amidst the freedom of college intercourse. This I have recommended, in another letter, with all the zeal of parental solicitude. Try as much as possible to have no disagreement, no contest with any one. "If it be possible, as much as lieth in you, live peaceably with all." For this purpose, let the tones of your voice, and your whole air and manner, be free from that rough, acrid, insolent character, which young men of ardent minds, and buoyant feelings, are so apt to exhibit; and which are the beginning of so many distressing quarrels and disgraceful affrays. It has been my privilege, in the course of a long life, to be acquainted with several public men, of eminent talents, deeply and constantly engaged in political affairs; and employed, for thirty or forty years together, in intercourse and collision with all sorts of men, from the most excellent to the most corrupt and vile. And yet, though not religious men, I have never heard of their giving or receiving a challenge to fight a duel; never known them to be involved in any feud or broil with any one; never seen them reduced to the necessity of defending themselves, either by the fist, the pen, or the tongue, from the ferocious attacks of ruffians. What was the reason of this? Not because they had less discernment to perceive the designs of opponents; or less sensibility to insult; or less regard to their own dignity and honour than they ought to have had; but because they were "swift to hear, slow to speak, slow to wrath;" because they had the faculty of "ruling their own spirits;" because they saw the evil of dissension afar off, and avoided its approaches; because their language and tones were habitually mild, and adapted to disarm and conciliate rather than to provoke; in short, because they acted upon the maxim of the wise physician, who tells us, *obsta principiis;* "an ounce of prevention is worth a pound of cure." This was the grand secret of such men going through life with peaceful, undisturbed dignity, beloved and confided in by the community, and constraining even the wicked to speak well of them.

But who has not seen many, in public and private life, of a very opposite character? Men of equal talents, and, in many respects, of equal integrity and moral worth; but so morbidly sensitive to all opposition, so liable to the sallies of ungovernable passion, so hasty and unguarded in speech, and so incapable of all sober calculation of consequences, that they were constantly involved in broils, and sometimes in conflicts of disgraceful and brutal violence. Such men are to be avoided almost as much as ferocious beasts. To speak to them is unsafe. To attempt to transact business with them requires all the vigilance and caution necessary in handling or approaching an exploding substance.

Let me exhort you, then, my dear sons, as soon as possible to learn the character of all your fellow students, and especially of those with whom you are associated in the same class. If you perceive any to be particularly forward, or likely on account of any popular qualities, to take the lead, scrutinize them with peculiar care. The moment you perceive any one to be profane, rude, vulgar, irritable, quarrelsome, or forward in plotting or executing mischief, however great his talents, mark him; have as little to do with him as possible; neither say nor do anything to provoke his resentment; but avoid him, speak not to him, or of him more than you can help. If he discovers a disposition to be intimate with you, do not repel him offensively; but let him see, by negative rather than positive indications, that you prefer the company of other associates. If you go to the room of a corrupt and disorderly fellow student; if you are found in his company, or partaking with him in any amusement, you may be unexpectedly implicated in some of his freaks or follies, in a manner as unmerited as painful. I have known one event of this kind to involve an innocent and worthy student in serious and lasting difficulty. Indeed I would carry my advice to avoid all intercourse with the corrupt and disorderly, so far as to say, with earnestness, never allow yourselves to mix with the crowd which seldom fails to rush together, when any affray, great or small, occurs, either in the campus or in the street. However great the assemblage, and however strong the impulse of curiosity, refrain, if you can summon so much resolution, from approaching the scene. If you are present, with the most innocent intentions in the world, and with the most entire original freedom possible from the leading actors in the scene, some unexpected nervous excitement on your part, some remark of a reckless and foolish bystander, some blow intended for another lighting on yourselves, may render the gratification of a momentary curiosity a source of serious and lasting calamity. Often, very often have I had reason to be thankful, that some providential occurrence, rather than my own wisdom, prevented my making one of a crowd in which, from apparently small beginnings, passions were unexpectedly inflamed, violence extended, and a number of individuals suddenly implicated, and perhaps fatally injured, who had no connection whatever with the original conflict. The truth is, such scenes ought to be just as carefully avoided as the track of a fearful tornado, when sweeping past our place of abode.

But, my dear sons, while you avoid, with the utmost vigilance, the company of such young men as I have described, and all contact with such scenes of violence as those to which I have referred, remember that social intercourse with your fellow students, when wisely conducted, is of great value, and may be made the source of essential benefits. I say, when wisely conducted; for there is here great need of judgment and caution. Be not in haste to form intimacies. Enlightened and safe friendship is a plant of slow growth. No wise young man will give his heart and his confidence to one with whom he is only slightly acquainted. He will not only scrutinize his character with care himself, but he will also carefully mark how the candidate for his favour is regarded and treated by the best judges, who have been longer and more intimately acquainted with him. Try, as far as possible, to select, as the objects of your confidence, some of the best talents and the best scholarship among your fellow students. From such, provided their moral and social qualities do not render them dangerous, you may expect to derive most pleasure, most intellectual excitement, most solid instruction. Guard against the error of having too many intimates. It frequently happens that sanguine, raw young men, find confidents in every place of their residence, whether for a longer or shorter time. Such confidential relations ought always to be very few, and very cautiously formed. He who makes them many will soon find himself betrayed and embarrassed. Not one friend in a thousand is fit to be entrusted with the private concerns of others, and especially with those personal secrets which it is the interest of every one to conceal from the public. Even where there is a strict sense of honour, essential weakness of character renders many a worthy individual an utterly unsafe depositary of confidential communications. I have met with but two or three friends in a long life whom I found it prudent thus to trust. You will be very fortunate if you meet with more than one in all your college.

But further, be not so intimate with any, as either to waste in social intercourse that time of your own which ought to be spent in study; or to encroach on their time in such a manner as to interrupt them in the performance of their duty. I have known some students so inconsiderate as to spend a portion of almost every day in going from room to room, visiting their fellow students. Such young men lessen their own dignity; make their visits cheap; waste their own time; and invade the time, the studies, and, of course, the comfort of others. Lord Bacon was accustomed, with emphasis, to say—"*Temporis fures amici.*" Cotton Mather, and, after him, Dr. Watts, caused to be inscribed, in large letters, over their study doors, these words—"BE SHORT." That student who spends much time in his social visits, gives ample evidence that he is neglecting his studies, and is likely to make a poor scholar. But this is not all: he will very soon become an unwelcome visitant to all, excepting those who are as indolent and reckless as himself.

In all your intercourse with your fellow students, adhere to the strictest principles of delicacy and honour. Never betray, or take the advantage of any confidence reposed in you. Never employ any indirect arts, or insidious means, to raise yourselves, or to depress others. Never allow yourselves to use any information or opportunity which your intimacy may give, either directly or indirectly, to the injury of one whom you call your friend. In short, I would say, never permit yourselves to make any use of the most unguarded disclosure, or of the most confidential conversation, which you would not be perfectly willing that all the world should know, and that all your friends should apply to yourselves. Begin now, my dear sons, when your social character is forming, to despise and hate everything like trick, deceit, or underhand management, in your intercourse with others; everything that shuns the light, or which, if known, would be considered as inconsistent with perfect fairness and candour. No one can tell how much of that which is now concealed, and which he supposed could never be known, may one day be unexpectedly dragged to light. Let the most entire sincerity, openness, and manly integrity shine in every part of your conversation and deportment. I should be greatly mortified if any of your companions should be able to say, that while professing to be his friend, you had taken the advantage of your intimacy, in the least tittle, to wound his reputation, or injure his feelings.

Nay, I would go one step further, and say, not only adhere to the strictest integrity and honour in all your intercourse with those whom you call your friends, and who you are willing should be so regarded; but also toward your opponents, and even your bitterest enemies. If the worst enemy I have in the world should, in an unguarded moment, utter in my hearing a speech which he did not deliberately intend to make, or disclose a fact which he earnestly wished to conceal, or drop from his pocket a private paper, which he was solicitous to keep from others—I should, in most cases, consider myself as bound in honour not to divulge them. Hence the unanimity with which all honourable people condemn the repeating of private conversation; and hence the severity with which all well constituted and delicate minds reprobate the conduct of the eavesdropper, who gains a knowledge of domestic secrets, or party plans, by mean, secret listening. If I can approach my enemy, or meet my opponent in open warfare, every honourable mind will justify me in doing so: but I would not for the world consent to be, or to employ, a spy, whom all civilized nations concur in sending to the gallows.

It is a maxim of policy with some students to seek and cultivate intimacies with such of their college companions as belong to the most wealthy and conspicuous families; accordingly, when a son of a President of the United States, or of a distinguished member of Congress, or of a citizen of great wealth enters college, it is considered as good policy by many calculating youth early to make their acquaintance, and to become, as far as possible, intimate with them. There is much less wisdom in this than is commonly supposed. The sons of such distinguished parents are seldom sober-minded and virtuous. They have been commonly too much accustomed to gaiety, and company, and dissipation, and luxurious living, to be either diligent students or good scholars. Their habits, too, are apt to be lax and expensive; and they too frequently betray into unlawful liberties and unexpected and inconvenient expenses, those who court their company; and, in the end, in nine cases out of ten, they cost much more than they profit us. The truth is, instead of seeking, anterior to inquiry and experience, peculiar intimacy with such young men, I should be more distrustful of such than of others; more afraid of their proffered friendship; more apprehensive of danger from being found much in their company; more careful to scrutinize the real stamp and bearing of their character, than if, with equally plausible appearances, they had more moderate claims, and had been brought up with more humble retiring simplicity. The sons of pious parents, and sometimes even of eminent ministers of the gospel, have, in some instances, turned out to be profligate, and proved pestiferous companions: but, on the other hand, young men trained in pious families, in regular habits, in plain and moderate expenditures, and with a reliance, under God, on their own efforts, for success in life, are, in general, the most safe and profitable associates, and, of course, most worthy of being selected as friends.

In short, I hope you will act in college as the wise and the virtuous act in the ordinary intercourses of society. Be on amicable and neighbourly terms with all, excepting the profligate and vile. With them have no intercourse that can possibly be avoided. Never visit them. Never be seen in their rooms or their company, however great their talents, or however eminent their scholarship. Let your selectest intimacies be with youth of the highest character for talents and attainments, provided their moral character be unblemished and pure, and especially, if they give evidence of sincere piety. Where there is true religion, there is something that is worthy of confidence, and that may always be made profitable to you, even though accompanied with only moderate intellectual powers, and medium scholarship.

I shall close this letter by putting you on your guard against a particular weakness which I have often observed to have a place, and to exert no small influence, among associates in college. I mean the cowardice and servility of those who feel as if they were bound to imitate their companions in everything; and as if all departure from this imitation were to be considered as so many marks of painful inferiority. Often—very often—have I known youthful members of college anxious to be like their classmates, and other associates, in everything; following the same fashions; going to the same places of resort; manifesting the same superiority to parental supervision and restraint; and mortified if they could not take the same liberties, and display the same independence in all their movements. This is so far from being a manly, independent spirit, that it is directly the reverse. It argues a weak dependence on others for giving law to our conduct. Is it manly or wise to follow the shadows of others, perhaps no more entitled to be a model than yourselves? If you do not follow their example, is it not quite as true that they do not follow yours? Besides, if you must be conformed, to the wishes of others, is it not much better that you should consult the judgment, and be regulated by the wishes of those who know you best, who love you most, who take a deeper interest in your welfare, and understand what will promote that welfare better than any others; than that you should follow in the wake of inexperienced, thoughtless companions, who are miserable judges of what is best either for you or themselves; who actually care nothing about your real welfare; and only wish to make you subservient to their present pleasure? I have been a thousand times both surprised and disgusted to find amiable and ingenuous youth, so cowardly and servile in their constant reference to the habits of their fellow students, that they were ready to break through the wishes, and even the authority of parents and guardians, for the sake of indulging this imitative spirit. Those who feel and act thus, may imagine that they manifest manliness and independence of character; but they were never more deceived. In the whole business they are displaying a childish reliance on the authority of children like themselves, as weak as it is mischievous.

LETTER XV.

LITERARY SOCIETIES IN COLLEGE.

Concordiâ res parvæ crescunt, discordiâ maximæ dilabuntur.
SALLUST.

Comes jucundus in viâ pro vehiculo est.—PUBL. SYR.

MY DEAR SONS—The "American Whig" and "Cliosophic" societies have long existed in the College of New Jersey, and have exerted no small influence on the improvement and character of its students. I will not trouble you now with any details of the history of those societies. You know that the great professed purpose of their institution was that they might promote some important objects, which the ordinary exercises of the college were not so well adapted to secure, particularly a spirit of fraternal friendship among the students, and also a laudable emulation in literature, science, manners, and morals. Such is the theory of these institutions; and if their actual administration had always been in faithful conformity with this theory, they would, no doubt, have produced fruits of far greater value than have been ever realized. But large allowance must always be made for the management of every association conducted by ardent young men, of little experience, of sanguine feelings, and of much self-confidence.

Still these societies are truly valuable, and worthy of encouragement; and it gives me pleasure to know that you are connected with one of them. My great design in referring to the subject, is to take an opportunity of urging upon you to prize this connection highly, and to study, by all the means in your power, to make it profitable to yourselves and all your fellow members.

You are aware of the evils which are apt to arise and to interfere both with the comfort and the usefulness of such associations among young men in college. The same evils which disturb all other society are apt, of course, to operate here. Beside these, there are many arising from the inexperience, the ardour, the rashness, the vanity, the pride, and the other passions of youth. It has been sometimes observed, that there are no disciplinarians more rigorous, and even intolerant than young men. But their rigour is apt to be spasmodic and unseasonable, and to be followed by paroxysms of indulgence, levity, irritation, disorder, and even violence far more revolting than their spasms of rigour. If the same members could continue to act for twenty or thirty years together, these evils would be gradually, but certainly diminished. This, however, cannot be the case. A constant succession of the raw, the ardent, and the inexperienced, are destined to be the counsellors and the guides in every measure.

The simple statement of these evils will itself go far toward furnishing an index both to their prevention and their correction. You ought to be continually learning in the hall of your society not only those lessons which will tend to your improvement in mental culture, and in literary acquirement and taste; but also in whatever is adapted to refine your moral and social feelings, and polish your manners. Here you ought continually to cherish that generous, fraternal emulation which seeks to excel, and, instead of sickening with envy at the talents and success of others, is stimulated by laudable efforts to overtake and surpass them. Here you ought to be constantly excited to higher and higher acquisitions in every intellectual accomplishment. Here it ought to be your aim, amidst all the diversities of temper, all the jarrings of youthful passion and all the ebullitions of ignorance, inexperience and rashness, to cherish with studious care the virtues of self-command, prudence, gentleness, and habitual respectfulness. The hall of your society may be regarded as a foretaste of what you are to meet with, on a greater scale, on the theatre of the world. It has been your fortune to be personally acquainted with some, who, amidst all the folly, the turbulence, the vulgarity, and the ill-manners of many with whom they came in contact, were never involved in any embarrassing quarrel, but steered through life with a remarkable exemption from feuds and animosities. And you have known others so morbidly touchy and inflammable themselves, and, at the same time, so regardless of the feelings of others, as to be perpetually involved in broils and conflicts wherever they went. Tempers and scenes of both these classes are not unknown even in the halls of literary societies. And I would earnestly exhort you to let your hall, whenever it may be opened, be a place of moral as well as intellectual discipline. To this end, the following counsels, I will venture confidently to say, are worthy of your serious consideration.

1. Faithfully resist the election of any member into your society who is known to be remarkable for his bad scholarship, his vulgar or immoral habits, or his insolent, perverse temper. Let no temptation of adding to your numbers induce you to vote for admitting any student of this character. Such persons, when unfortunately introduced, seldom fail to give more trouble than they are worth. They weaken and degrade, rather than strengthen any society to which they belong; and sometimes have been known, by their vulgar, profligate insolence, to inflict lasting disgrace, and all but ruin on the body with which they were connected. Let nothing deter you from opposing their introduction. Do it mildly; do it in guarded language; and if no other method be likely to succeed, propose respectfully a committee of inquiry, and inform that committee

confidentially of the reasons of your opposition. If this were faithfully done, no one can estimate the happy influence which might thereby be exerted on the character of a band of students.

2. Be perfectly punctual in your attendance on all the meetings of the society to which you belong, and perform with diligence and fidelity every task which its rules may impose upon you. Never either neglect or slight any exercise which it becomes your duty to perform. That which is worth doing at all is worth doing well. To refuse the time and labour necessary to its execution in the best manner, is doing injustice to your fellow members, as well as cheating yourselves. If the principles of the society are not faithfully carried into execution, it might as well, nay better, be disbanded.

3. Make a point of addressing all your fellow members with politeness and respect. Let your hall, so far as you are concerned, be a school of the strictest urbanity and respectfulness. Let no opposite tone or conduct on the part of others tempt you for a moment to deviate from this course. "A soft answer turneth away wrath." Nothing tends more directly to disarm passion or insolence than either a dignified silence in some cases, and in others a rigid observance of the laws of urbanity and respectfulness. I know it is your desire to avoid all those feuds, broils, and scenes of violence which are so apt to grow out of youthful animosities, and which are too frequently followed by results as criminal as they are silly and contemptible. It is impossible to measure the happy influence which one member of such a society, whose example is perfectly correct and gentlemanly, may impart to all his fellow members.

4. Endeavour, by all the means in your power, to render the society to which you belong, a source of discipline in morals, as well as in literary and scientific improvement. Remember that you are bound by the principles of your institution to frown upon all disorder and immorality, as well as upon bad scholarship,

and intellectual negligence. Of course, no student, known to be habitually immoral, ought to be admitted into your society; and whenever it becomes apparent, that any one who has been admitted is immoral, he ought immediately to be suspended, and if he persists in his delinquency, he ought to be forthwith expelled. A few such examples would do a literary society essential good; would do more to elevate its character, and in the end, to add to its numbers, than could well be told. Let every member recollect, that a large portion of the trust for keeping the society, to which he belongs, in this state of moral health, is committed to him; and that he can do more by bearing a faithful testimony, from time to time, in favour of moral correctness, than he would easily believe. By throwing out proper sentiments on this subject upon all suitable occasions, and by voting for strict discipline in all cases of delinquency, each one may become a conservator of the moral character, and consequently, of the true honour of the society, to an extent which invests every member with a mighty power of doing good.

5. You are aware that most of the literary societies in colleges avail themselves of the principle of secrecy, to increase curiosity and interest in their favour. Whether this feature in their constitutions is dictated by wisdom, and confers any real advantage, is a question which I do not think proper now to discuss. No one, however, of correct and honourable feelings can doubt for a moment that, as long as this principle is actually incorporated in the plan of any society to which he belongs, he is bound strictly and delicately to adhere to it, and to avoid everything which borders on an infringement of it. Nay, more; if any of the secrets of a rival society should by any means become known to you, my judgment is, that true delicacy of sentiment ought to prevent you from divulging them to a human being. If a son of mine, after accidentally becoming possessed of such secrets, were to disclose them, I should consider him as dishonoured.

6. Guard with sacred care against a spirit of carping and animosity toward a rival society. This is a very mischievous evil. The beginning of it is like the letting out of water. It generates strife. It occupies time which ought to be reserved for higher and better objects. And in some cases it has grown to a mass of mischief which no one anticipated, and over which all mourned. Evils of this kind, every one sees afterwards, might easily have been prevented by a small measure of coolness and prudence in the beginning. I firmly believe that the most of those disagreements which have interfered with amicable and pleasant co-operation in public festive services between rival societies, have arisen either from the littleness of punctilio, or from the equally censurable littleness of false honour, and weak jealousy, which ought to have no place in elevated minds.

7. But especially be careful in no case to allow your society to set itself against the authority of the college. This is like a civil war in the state, always to be avoided at almost any sacrifice. Even when the authority of the college is manifestly acting under an entire mistake in regard to facts, there may be, without impropriety, calm statements, and even respectful remonstrance; but in no case an attempt to exercise counter authority. Any society in a literary institution which should attempt this, in any form, ought instantly to be dissolved. A faculty would be wanting to itself, and unfaithful to the institution committed to its care, which should suffer such a rebellious society to exist for a single hour.

8. I will only add, let it be your constant study to render the society to which you belong as respectable, as useful, and as happy as possible. It has been delightful to observe how some individuals have endeared themselves to the society to which they belonged, by an amiable gentlemanly deportment; by a faithful discharge of all the duties which they owed to it; by embracing every opportunity of promoting its best interests,

and adding to its true honour. In the records of every such society you always find a few names handed down as benefactors from one generation of students to another. Let it be your study thus to transmit your own names with honour to coming times.

LETTER XV.

DRESS.

———"Of outward form
Elaborate, of inward less exact."—MILTON.

MY DEAR SONS—There are two extremes in regard to dress into which I have observed that college students are apt to fall. The one is a total negligence of it, leading to a disgusting slovenliness; the other a degree of scrupulous attention to it, which indicates foppery and dandyism. It is my earnest desire that none of my sons may fall into either of these extremes. And let it be remembered that they are both peculiarly apt to be adopted by students who board and lodge together in the same public edifice. There is something in the gregarious principle, which while it is productive of much good, is by no means unattended with serious evil.

Some good scholars, and young men otherwise entirely exemplary, have been notoriously slovenly in their dress. But it was a real blemish in their character, and was connected with no little disadvantage. It is no disgrace to a student to be poor; to be obliged to wear a threadbare, and even a patched garment. It is rather to his honour, and ought to be so felt by him, to be strictly economical; to dress according to his circumstances; and never to purchase new clothes until he is able honestly to pay for them. He who does otherwise is really the mean and dishonest man. But let not his economical dress be slouching or filthy. Let him not walk about among his fellows, for hours after rising, with his shoes down at the heel, with his stockings hanging loose about his legs; or any part of his clothing visibly begrimed with dirt. Cleanliness and neatness are among the moral virtues, and can never be neglected by any one with impunity. We have no more right to render our persons disgusting to those who approach us, than we have to mutilate and enfeeble them. It is a duty, however scanty or old our garments may be, to see that they be neat and clean, and that our persons be kept, according to the best of our ability, in a manner evincing decency and care. I have sometimes seen young men passing through the corridors of college, and entering the recitation rooms, and even the prayer-hall, with their dress so broken, slovenly and dirty, as manifested little respect either for their instructors, or the God whom they professed to worship, or even for themselves.

But there is another extreme against which every student ought to be put on his guard. I mean that of inordinate and idolatrous attention to dress, which manifests the expenditure of much time and money on the object, and which designates the fop and the dandy. The wise youth, the real gentleman, will always try to dress in such a manner as not to draw attention at all to his dress. His only study will be to have it always so plain, simple, neat, and becoming his character, as that no one will find occasion to take special notice of it. Happily you are not able to dress in a profuse and expensive manner. The circumstances of your father forbid your indulging yourselves in that ornate and splendid costume to which perhaps your inclination, if unrestrained, might lead. But if I were ever so wealthy, my judgment would be against allowing you to indulge in costly and extravagant adorning of the body, which is criminal in itself, and which seldom fails to mark the frivolous mind. I never knew a diligent student, a really good scholar, to indulge in this habit; and whenever I see a young man falling into it, I always involuntarily set him down in my own mind as a poor trifler.

If you ask me, where is the harm of indulging in showy and expensive habits of dress? I answer, it must occupy a large share of time and attention, which ought to be bestowed on better objects; and hence those students who are distinguished by ostentatious and expensive clothing are never good scholars. It would be almost encroaching on the province of a miracle if they were. But this is not all. This habit is adapted to do mischief among their fellow students. Those who cannot afford, and ought not to attempt to indulge in the same habit, are often tempted to imitate it, and thus their parents become unnecessarily involved in an expense altogether inconvenient and perhaps distressing. By this means the cost of a college education is greatly increased, and placed beyond the reach of many who might otherwise enjoy it. Nor is this the worst effect. By emulating the habits in this respect of the sons of the wealthy, the sons of those in less affluent circumstances are tempted, contrary to the laws of the college, to get that upon improper credit, which they were not able to pay for, and which ought never to have been gotten at all, and thus shut themselves up to the distressing and humiliating dilemma, of either bringing an unauthorized and burdensome debt on their parents; or of ultimately defrauding the tradesman who was weak enough, or wicked enough to give them credit. If there be any student so unprincipled as to reply, that he does not feel bound to regard such considerations—that he cares for nothing but his own comfort—be it known to such an one, that he stands on substantially the same ground with the burglar and the highwayman, who act upon the principle of consulting their own comfort at the expense of others, which is, in fact, the vital spirit of all crime.

There is another fault in regard to dress, of which I cannot help expressing strong reprobation. I mean the disposition manifested by some to wear fantastic dresses, not particularly expensive, perhaps not so expensive as many plainer and more simple garments;

but whimsical, queer, and adapted to excite ridicule wherever they are seen. I remember one young man, who, a number of years ago, appeared in our college campus, and in our streets, in a dress of the most ridiculous kind. Wherever he went he attracted the notice, and excited the laughter of all classes. This seemed to gratify him; for he was incapable of attaining any more laudable distinction; and he persisted in wearing the garment for a considerable time. He was hissed, and all but insulted by the boys in the streets, and might have been involved in serious broils with his assailants, had he not, fortunately, possessed a baby-like weakness, rather than an irritable or pugnacious temperament. It is easy to conceive how such a dress might involve its wearer in perpetual difficulty, and even in fatal conflicts.

It is well known, that in some literary institutions there is a prescribed dress, or uniform, in which all its pupils daily appear, and which it is not lawful to lay aside, excepting in vacation, when absent from the institution, or, at any rate, exempt from its rules. There appear to me to be some very substantial advantages in this regulation. In the first place, it promotes economy; for the prescribed dress is always plain, simple, cheap, and easily procured, and when obtained by wholesale, for large numbers, will be, of course, reduced in price. Secondly, it destroys that expensive emulation in dress, to which I have before referred, as so full of mischief. As all must dress alike, it leaves no room for ostentatious display. And thirdly, where this rule is in operation, all the students of the institution are known by their costume; so that the moment they are seen, they can be distinguished from all others. This appears to me an effect of no small importance. I have always considered it as highly desirable that the pupils of any institution should be distinguishable at all times, day and night, from the youth of the surrounding population. It operates as a restraint, as a safeguard, and has, doubtless, prevented a thousand mischiefs, which would otherwise have occurred, and been the means of dragging to light a thousand more which might have been for ever hidden from human view.

For myself, I have always regretted that the old practice of wearing the black gown in the recitation room, in the chapel, and on all public occasions, has been laid aside by the students of Nassau Hall, and I believe, by those of most other colleges in the United States. In our commencement exercises alone, if I mistake not, this appendage is retained; and in some other colleges it is, even on these occasions, discarded. This is, in my opinion, an improvement the backward way. I have no doubt that this particular costume had, when it was worn, a beneficial effect on the feelings of the individual who wore it; that it led him to recollect his responsibility; to feel that he was observed, and to maintain a deportment growing out of this feeling. Nor can I hesitate to believe, that an impression was made by it on the minds of others by no means without profit. Forms may be carried so far as to eat out all substance; but it is also true, that they may be so far abandoned as to carry all refinement and decorum, and especially all dignity, with them.

LETTER XVII.

CARE OF THE STUDENT'S ROOM.

"He who can sit with comfort in a disorderly room, cannot have an orderly mind."—ANON.

MY DEAR SONS—The maxim of the lawyers, *De minimis non curat lex*, though wise and applicable in juridical matters, is not equally safe and sound in many of the affairs of common life, and especially in the large department of human conduct, comprehended under the general title of personal manners and habits. The comfort of ordinary life depends much less upon great actions and movements, which occur only now and then, than on the minor concerns of temper, language and order, which belong to every hour, and exert an influence on all the enjoyments of life.

The maintenance of perfect order, in the apartment which you occupy, is a matter of more importance, and has a more direct bearing on your comfort, and even your success in study, than you would, at first view, imagine. So deep is my persuasion of this, that I am induced to make it the subject of a distinct but brief letter, which, I trust, will be sufficiently interesting, in your view, to engage your serious attention.

If the motto which stands at the head of this letter be considered as expressing a correct sentiment, then the subject of it ought not to be regarded as a trivial matter. That which either indicates a disorderly mind, or which is adapted to increase and perpetuate this evil, surely ought to be avoided with studious care. Many people judge of a student by the appearance of his room: and certainly when it lies in disorder and dirt, no favourable estimate of his character can possibly be drawn from it.

It is possible that some students who affect slovenliness in their dress, as an evidence that they are too much absorbed in study to think of their persons, may affect the same carelessness in regard to the apartments which they occupy. I will not pronounce all such appearances the result of mere affectation; but, beyond all doubt, they mark a lamentable defect of character, and cannot fail to deduct seriously from both the comfort and the usefulness of the individual to whom they belong.

A disorderly and unclean apartment is unfriendly to the comfortable and uninterrupted pursuit of study. The physical inconvenience to which it gives rise, can scarcely fail to interfere with a pleasant flow of mental thought. When books are out of their proper places; when all the means of study are in disorder, it would be strange, indeed, if the operations of the mind could proceed in as smooth and unobstructed a manner as if the external circumstances were different.

Make a point, then, of keeping everything in your study in a state of perfect neatness and regularity. Whether your books be few or many, keep them in their proper places, and in perfect order. Let all your manuscripts be so arranged as that you shall be able to lay your hand upon any one of them in a moment. Tie your pamphlets in bundles, in a certain order, understood by yourself, and as soon as may be get them bound in convenient volumes. Fold, label, and deposit in proper drawers, all loose papers, so as to be at no loss to find any one of them whenever called for. And in general, let everything in your study bear the marks of order, system, and perfect neatness. You can have no conception, without having made the experiment, how much time and trouble will be saved by the adoption of this plan. When you are tempted to think that you have not time to put a book or paper, which you have been using, into its proper place, ask yourselves whether it may not cost you an hour or more afterwards to search for that, which half a minute would have sufficed to deposit in its appropriate situation. Let me advise you also to preserve and file copies of all your letters, and especially those on any kind of business; and when you cannot find time for this, to keep at least a distinct memorandum of the dates, principal contents, conveyance, &c., of all such letters. You will, in the end, save more time by this regularity than you can now easily imagine. Among the many omissions in my early life, I have a thousand times lamented my having omitted, for many years, to keep copies of my business letters, and to preserve and file, in proper order, other important papers, so as to have them accessible at any time without the loss of a moment. How much time I have lost, and how much trouble I have incurred by this failure, no arithmetic at my command can calculate.

Some of the most eminent men, for wisdom and usefulness, that the world has ever seen, were remarkable for their attention to the subject of this letter. Washington, the father of his country, from his early youth, was distinguished for his perfect method and neatness in everything. During the whole of his public life, we are told, he was punctual in filing and labeling every paper, however small, or apparently trivial, which related to any concern or act of his life; even notes of ceremony; not knowing what measure of importance any such paper might afterwards assume. So that no written document could be called for, relating to his official life, which he could not at any time produce.

Let no student say, that his papers can never be so important as were those of Washington; and that, therefore, there cannot be the same inducement to preserve, and keep them in order. It is, indeed, by no means probable that your papers will be as important to the public, as those of that illustrious man were; but they may be of quite as much importance to yourself; and no man can tell of how much interest they may be to your country. Peculiar and unexpected circumstances may invest them with a degree of importance which you cannot now anticipate. At any rate, disposing them in proper and convenient order, and depositing them where they may be found in a moment, will occupy but little time, and may, long afterwards, serve purposes which you little imagined.

The celebrated Mr. Whitefield, that "prince of preachers," in the last century, was greatly distinguished, from early life, for neatness in his person, for order in his apartment, and for regular method in his affairs. He was accustomed to say, that a minister should be "without spot;" and remarked, on one occasion, that he could not feel comfortable, if he knew that his gloves were out of their proper place. The advantages of establishing such habits are too numerous to be specified. They save time; and the degree of comfort they give cannot be easily measured.

The biographers of the late celebrated Mr. Wilberforce tell us, that that great and good man was rather remarkably careless in regard to regularity and order in his study. While he was indefatigably diligent in his labours for the public, his books and papers were always in disorder, lying in heaps, and frequently giving rise to perplexity and delay, in searching for that which was wanted. On more than one occasion, important papers, when called for by some of the most elevated persons in the kingdom, were out of their proper place, and not to be found; which gave rise to an agitation and loss of time not a little painful.

Good farmers and mechanics tell us, that it is important to have "a place for everything, and everything in its place." This maxim is quite as applicable and important to the student as to any one else. The punctual observance of it not only saves time, as the slightest consideration will evince, but it tends to preserve tranquillity of mind; and what in many cases is still more important, it may prevent the entire loss of papers, books, or other articles left out of their proper places.

LETTER XVIII.

EXPENSES.

"Φειδεο των κτεανων.'

"Suum cuique."

My Dear Sons—It is well known that the greater part of the students in our colleges belong to families in very moderate, and not a few of them in straitened circumstances, insomuch that many of them find it extremely difficult to meet the expenses of the institution; and to some it would be impossible without the aid of charitable funds. If we could go through all the classes in these institutions, and examine the real circumstances of each individual, we should find many parents subjecting themselves and their families to the most pinching economy, really denying themselves some comforts, which many would call indispensable, for the sake of sustaining their sons through a course of education. In other cases we should see sons subjecting themselves to a rigour of economy truly severe, and which, if it could be generally known, would be regarded as at once marvellous and honourable, as marking extraordinary decision of character.

While this is the case with one class of students, there is another whose course belongs to the opposite extreme. Their supplies of money are abundant. In consequence of this they are profuse and wasteful. Some are permitted, and even encouraged by unwise parents, to indulge in habits of unnecessary expense; and others, stimulated by this example, but less able to follow it, in spite of every charge that can be given them to the contrary, give way to those habits, and recklessly incur debts which prove greatly oppressive to their parents, and sometimes plunge them into serious difficulties. This latter class of students may be considered as the pests of all literary institutions; and, next to the grossly immoral and profligate, (with whom indeed, they are too often very closely connected) the means of the greatest injury to their fellow students. When a student has much money in his pocket, or feels confident that he can rely on receiving what he wishes, the mischiefs arising from this source are so multiplied, and so very serious, that it is wonderful wealthy parents will ever allow their children to be laden with such a curse.

The mischiefs growing out of this "plethora of the pocket" to the students themselves who possess it, are more injurious and deplorable than any one would imagine who had not personally watched the process of such things. He who has money to spend, will, of course, have objects to spend it upon; and these objects will certainly be, to a great extent, hurtful. He will seldom fail to indulge himself in extra eating and drinking, which, from their unwholesome nature, as well as from their leading to excess in quantity, will frequently, if not always, do more or less harm to his health. To load the stomach with confectionery, and other luxuries; to eat hot suppers over and above all ordinary meals; to indulge in every rare and expensive viand, adapted to stimulate the appetite, and eventually to bring on a morbid state of the system;—these are the habits which every young man who is flush of money is tempted to form; and that their influence must be morbid and unhappy, and may lead to fatal diseases, no one who reflects on the subject can doubt. But these evils are not the whole of the mischief to be apprehended. The vices of students are commonly social. In partaking of their luxurious meals and other indulgences, they are fond of having companions; and they take pride in imparting of their plenty in this respect, gratuitously, to those who are not so plentifully provided with the means of indulgence. This extends the mischief in two ways. It increases the number of those who are ensnared and injured; and it tempts both parties, by the influence of the gregarious principle, to eat and drink more than either would alone.

Nor is this all. Those who are placed under no stint with regard to money, are tempted to be dissipated; to neglect their studies; to be arrogant and assuming; to indulge themselves in various irregular practices, unfriendly to study, and adapted to betray them into various forms of disorderly conduct. All experience testifies that such students are usually the most disorderly in the institution;—very seldom even tolerable scholars,—and so, frequently the subjects of painful and disreputable discipline, and these unhappy results may be confidently calculated upon the moment any young man appears with a plentiful supply of money in his pocket.

You have reason to be thankful, my dear sons, that the comparative poverty of your father cuts you off from these temptations. And I hope you consider this circumstance as a real advantage rather than the contrary. Still allow me to put you on your guard against some temptations, which, notwithstanding this restriction on your means, may sometimes assail you.

1. Never be ashamed of your narrow circumstances. Never affect to have money at will. Never allow your wealthy fellow students to imagine that you envy them, or that you wish to emulate their dress, their appearance, and their liberality of expenditure. I have sometimes felt regret and mortification to see students, who in intellectual and moral worth stood among the very first of their classes, who struggled to appear as well dressed as their wealthier companions, and seemed to give way to a painful sense of inferiority if they

were unable to do it. There is a littleness in this of which a high-minded youth ought to be ashamed. Some of the most eminent and highly honoured men that the world ever saw, commenced their career in absolute poverty, and, what was much to their credit, were never ashamed in their highest advancement, to recollect and advert to their humble origin. Nay more, there was every reason to believe that their poverty, instead of being a disadvantage, was the stimulus which urged them on to diligence in study—to the highest efforts of which they were capable, and to ultimate greatness. It was, under God, the making of them.

2. Never accept of the gratuitous offers of your moneyed fellow students to share their luxuries with them, or to partake, at their expense, in any extra food or drink, or in any extra amusement, whether lawful or not, in which they may solicit you to accompany them. It is not safe to associate much with such students. It may expose you either to real disorder, or, at any rate, to the suspicion of the faculty, either of which ought to be sacredly avoided. There is also something painful to me, and I presume to every ingenuous mind, in being indebted to the bounty of such a young man for any enjoyment. Very few such young men have any real magnanimity; and they may imagine hereafter that you are their debtors, and feel as if you ought to recognize this debt, and be ready to return or acknowledge it. I have known gratuities of this kind to be cast in the teeth of those who consented to receive them, years afterwards, and to inflict not a little mortification. Never accept such gratuities. Whenever and by whomsoever offered, decline them with the respectfulness and urbanity of gentlemen, but with inflexible firmness.

3. Never purchase anything that is not indispensable, while matters absolutely necessary remain unprovided for. What would you think of a student who should expend twenty or thirty dollars for a splendid set of books, which he could easily do without, while he had not wherewithal to pay his daily board, or to dis-

charge his bill for necessary clothing? Let the honest principle, of giving to every one and to every claim what is justly due, and making a corresponding calculation in all your expenditures, at all times, and throughout life, govern you.

4. Never think of obtaining on credit what you have not the cash to pay for at the moment; especially never consent thus to obtain that which is a mere luxury, and which, of course, you can do without. I have personally known students, who were the sons of parents in very moderate and even straitened circumstances, who had so little self-command, that, when their pockets were empty, they would obtain on credit mere luxuries, and sometimes those of a very expensive kind; and, perhaps, at the end of a session, had a bill brought in, the amount of which astonished themselves, and greatly incommoded their parents. The practice of purchasing on credit, articles which are not necessary, is one which the wise, with one consent, agree in denouncing. It not only leads to all the evils just alluded to, but also to another no less serious. Those who purchase on credit must expect to pay considerably more for a given article than those who pay the cash. The seller who disposes of his property in this way always calculates on losing a considerable portion of the whole by delinquent debtors. To meet and cover this loss, his plan is to add a certain percentage to the price of the article which he sells on credit; so that the pockets of his punctual debtors are taxed to help him meet the loss sustained by his delinquent ones. My solemn advice, therefore, would be that you never, especially now in your minority, purchase the smallest article on credit. If it be a mere luxury, not strictly speaking needed for your health or comfort, you ought not to purchase it at all, even if you had the money in your pocket. But even if it be a necessary of life, you ought to postpone the purchase of it as long as you can, to avoid the payment of a double price for it.

The mischiefs arising from the students of our college purchasing on credit, and suffering bills against them to appear with unexpected accumulation at the end of each session, has proved so crying an evil, and has been followed with so many consequences injurious to the students themselves, and to their parents, that the trustees of the college have repeatedly and strongly remonstrated against the practice, and have even gone so far as to entreat the parents of their pupils not to pay the bills for articles obtained by minors, on credit, contrary to the public notice and injunction of the college government. Nay, under a deep impression of the importance of the subject, the Legislature of the state of New Jersey has passed an act, forbidding any person in the neighbourhood of the college to give credit to any of its students, excepting for articles of absolute necessity, and making all such bills, in the case of minors, irrecoverable by law.

Many a young man, as I before said, whose circumstances were straitened, and who found it difficult to meet the expenses of his education, has been, notwithstanding, in the end, among the most respected and beloved of his class, far more so than the most wealthy. And this will never fail to be the case with any student in whose character the following circumstances unite. First, if he be among the first for scholarship. Secondly, if to his accomplishments in this respect he add the dignity, polish, and amiableness of a Christian gentleman; and, thirdly, if he make it appear, by all his deportment and habits, that he knows how to estimate at its real value that tinsel importance which wealth alone can give. I once knew a young man who was the most indigent individual in his class. But he was, at the same time, the best scholar, and the most amiable, polished, and well-bred gentleman of the whole number. The consequence may easily be imagined. He was felt and acknowledged to be the master spirit of the class. All did him homage.

You see, then, how important it is that all orderly

students, and all well-wishers to the college, should guard with sacred care against everything approaching to an infringement of this rule, fortified by a civil enactment. It is not only their duty to avoid everything of this kind on their own account, but also for the sake of example, and to co-operate in carrying into effect a regulation so vitally important to the comfort and prosperity of the college.

I hope, my dear sons, that, as faithful alumni of the institution to which you owe allegiance, and as sincere patriots, you wish to act in this whole matter of expense, in such a manner as shall tend to promote on a large scale, the welfare of your *Alma Mater*, and the great interests of knowledge and order in the community. It is easy to see that everything which tends to increase expense in the college must exert an unhappy influence in a variety of ways. Wealthy parents do not consider as they ought, that when their sons indulge in expensive dress, and appear able, from day to day, to gratify their taste by larger expenditure than the most of their companions in study can afford, they excite uncomfortable feelings in the minds of some less liberally supplied than themselves; they tempt others, who have not the means, to endeavour to vie with them in appearance and expenditure; they render the college a less eligible and pleasant place for indigent students; and perhaps, prevent some of this character from ever becoming members of the institution. In this way it is that by every violation of wise rules and principles, the great interests of knowledge and order in the whole community are seriously injured.

I take for granted that some of these considerations will appear altogether too refined and abstract to have any weight on the minds of many of your fellow students. Each one will be ready to say—"Am I my brother's keeper? It is enough for every one to take care of his own claims and interests." Is this the language or the spirit of dutiful sons, when weighing the claims and the interests of their beloved *Alma Mater?* Is this the language or spirit of young patriots, who consider it as a privilege and an honour, as well as a duty, to promote the great cause of knowledge and virtue in every department of the community? I can only say, if there be any who feel thus and speak thus, they manifest a narrowness of view, and a miserable selfishness, of which a rational and accountable creature, and especially one in a course of liberal education, and training for the duties and responsibilities of public life ought to be ashamed.

The situation of your father, of course, renders it impossible for you to think of emulating the expensive indulgences of some of your companions in study. I trust, my dear sons, this circumstance will not give rise to one moment's pain, nor lead you to feel as if they were, on this account, your superiors. If it has imposed upon you some salutary restraints; if it has excited you to more diligence in study, and more unwearied efforts to cultivate, enlarge, and strengthen your own minds—you have rather reason to rejoice than to mourn that your father is not a rich man. Never give way to the thought that money makes the man; or that mammon can be weighed in the scale against scholarship and virtue. What though you wear less expensive garments, and have less money to waste on injurious indulgences than some of your classmates? If you stand at the head of your associates in literary and scientific attainments, and maintain that high reputation as young gentlemen of integrity, urbanity, and honour to which I trust you will ever aspire, you may rely on it that the son of the proudest nabob, if he have no other distinction than that which his wealth gives him, will feel himself an inferior in your presence.

LETTER XIX.

ALMA MATER.

Jubemus te salvere, Mater!—PLAUTUS.

My Dear Sons—You are aware that the technical title which the dutiful and grateful son of a college gives to his literary parent, is *Alma Mater*. The word *alma* primarily conveys the idea of cherishing or nourishing, but it may also be considered as signifying holy, fair, benign, pure. And I take for granted that every *alumnus* of such an institution, who has acted the part of a dutiful son while under her care, and who has received from her that faithful and affectionate training which is never withheld from the docile and the reverential pupil, will be ever ready to say of his literary parent, with all the delightful emotions of filial respect and gratitude—"*Alma Mater! Sit semper florens, semper honoratissima, semper beata!*"

It is a maxim in common life, that when any young man manifests no respect for his mother, the conclusion is irresistible;—either that she is unworthy, or that he is a brute. If this is always the case with a mother according to the flesh, the maxim holds, with equal uniformity, and with equal force, in regard to a literary parent. Whenever you meet with an *alumnus* of a college who manifests no affection, no respect for the institution in which he has been trained, you may generally take for granted, without inquiring further, that he is an unworthy son, who during his connection with her, acted so undutiful a part as to embitter all his own recollections of that connection; and to leave no impression on her mind which she can remember but with pain.

The duties which a faithful son owes to a worthy mother are so many, and at the same time so obvious, that it may seem unnecessary to recount them. Yet as the duties due to literal mothers, plain and indubitable as they are, are too often forgotten and neglected by unworthy children according to the flesh; so the obligations by which educated young men are bound to their literary mothers are so seldom duly recognized or faithfully discharged, that a brief allusion to some of them is by no means a superfluous task.

1. The first duty which every *alumnus* of a college owes to his *Alma Mater* is to recognize his obligation to her, and to cherish those sentiments of respect, veneration, and gratitude, to which she is entitled at his hands. This obligation is real and deep, and ought ever to be remembered and acknowledged. Every young man who has passed, or is passing through a course of study in a literary institution, who has been faithfully instructed, and made the subject of wholesome parental discipline, is deeply indebted to that institution, and ought to cherish a strong and permanent impression of his debt. What though he may be able to see faults in his literary mother? What though some parts of her discipline may have been painful to him? Yet his obligation is not thereby destroyed, or even impaired. The probability is, that he, and not the college, was to blame for every penalty that fell upon him, for every frown which she manifested toward him; nay, that every act of severity which gave him temporary pain, and of which he may be sometimes ready to make complaint, was demanded by fidelity to his best interest, and, instead of diminishing, does but increase his obligation.

I hope, then, my dear sons, that wherever you may sojourn or settle in future life, in the exercise of a true filial spirit, you will cherish a strong and lively sense of obligation to your *Alma Mater*. Whatever may be

said of her defects, she has been a faithful mother to you. For every frown you may have received from her, for every rod of correction she may have inflicted upon you, instead of being offended, you ought to feel more deeply her debtors. And this debt, it will be equally pleasant to her, and honourable to yourselves, ever to bear in mind, and gratefully to acknowledge as long as you live. Whenever I find a student greatly attached to the college in which he is pursuing his studies, or after he has left it, cherishing a strong filial spirit toward it, I involuntarily adopt conclusions favourable to his character as a son. I take for granted that he has been a dutiful, diligent, and orderly student; that his connection with his *Alma Mater* was creditable to himself, as well as pleasant to her; and that every word he utters in her favour ought to be considered as redounding to his own honour.

2. If you are thus indebted to your *Alma Mater*, ought you not to abhor the thought of destroying her property, or doing anything that can possibly tend to her injury? The most wonderful infatuation concerning this point seems to possess the minds of many members of our colleges. When they become dissatisfied on any account with their instructors, one of the first things they think of is to wreak their vengeance on some portion of the college property; to destroy or deface some part of the public edifices, or their furniture. This, they imagine, will most effectually spite and mortify the faculty, the object of their resentment. But there never was a more miserable misapprehension, or a more fiend-like and malignant spirit. The property of the institution is all vested in the board of trustees, the legal curators of all her interests. Of course, when injury is done to any of these interests, it falls, not on the faculty, but on the college; impairing her strength, diminishing her power of doing good, and of course rendering her, so far as the injury goes, less of a blessing to the community.

What would be thought of a young man, who, when

his literal mother, after a long course of labour and toil for his benefit, had reproved him for some gross fault, should wreak his vengeance on her dwelling and furniture, destroying or defacing everything within his reach; thus doing all in his power to vex and injure her whom he was bound upon every principle to honour and cherish? He would be pronounced an ungrateful, infatuated demon, setting at defiance, at once, every dictate of reason, duty, self-interest, and self-respect, for the gratification of a blind and brutal passion.

Equally infatuated and demon-like is that student, who, when by his own folly and wickedness he has subjected himself to merited and most righteous discipline, undertakes to resent it, and to give expression to his anger, not by assailing the persons of those who have offended him, which he knows would subject him to still heavier discipline, but by attacking the property of the institution, by subjecting to serious loss those from whom he has never received anything but benefits.

Still less apology than even for these, can be made for those who, without any provocation, are in the habit, from mere wantonness, of cutting and otherwise defacing the benches, doors, window-frames, fences, &c., of the college, rendering them odious in their appearance, and, in many cases, altogether unfit for use. Is this the conduct which becomes dutiful children, who know that to injure their mother is to injure themselves? Ever remember, my dear sons, not only that the property of the college is not yours but hers, and, of course, that you have no right to injure it in the least degree; but that your right to injure it is even less than if you were its rightful owner. If it were your own, you might, indeed, do as you pleased with it; but as it is not your own, you ought to exercise a far more scrupulous care not to injure it than if it were. But even more than this; it belongs to a moral parent, to whom you are deeply indebted, and whom to injure is even more unreasonable and more criminal than if you stood to her in no such relation.

3. Another duty which you now owe, and will ever owe to your *Alma Mater*, is to be jealous, and scrupulously careful of her good name and honour. If the sons of a great literary parent are not jealous of her reputation, and do not stand forth as the advocates of her fame, who can be expected to do it? Let no *alumnus* say of his *Alma Mater* that he cannot conscientiously praise her; that she is far from being what he could wish. To whom does it belong to try to improve her condition, and raise her character, but to her sons? To withhold their praise, when they have not done all in their power to render her worthy of it, is as ignoble as it is unjust. This consideration leads me to say,

4. That you are bound to study and endeavour, to the end of life, to do all in your power to elevate, strengthen, enrich, and adorn your *Alma Mater* in all her interests. In this respect it is certain that the habits of our ancestors were far more favourable to literature than those of the present day. Several centuries ago, it was common for eminent and wealthy men in the old world to exercise splendid munificence toward the seminaries of learning in which they were trained, or which became, on any ground, objects of their favour. They erected large and splendid edifices for libraries and halls; gave ample endowments for their support; founded professorships and scholarships; established bursaries and premiums for the encouragement of pupils; and in various ways contributed to extend, strengthen and adorn the nurseries of knowledge. Almost all the principal buildings, and most sumptuous foundations in the universities of the old world, and especially of Great Britain, were established, not by the universities themselves, out of their own funds, but by munificent individuals, many of whom have by this laudable liberality transmitted their names with honour to posterity. Nor has this praiseworthy practice been unknown in our own country. The friends of Harvard University in Massachusetts,

have set the noblest example of this kind hitherto presented on this side of the Atlantic. The names of Harvard, and Hollis, and Hancock, and Hersey, and Erving, to say nothing of several still more munificent later patrons, are all worthy of honourable commemoration. It is to be lamented that this species of liberality has been, in a great measure, confined to the single state of Massachusetts. For although a few cases have occurred, both in the West and the South, of large endowments to literary institutions, yet they have been indeed "few and far between;" whereas they have occurred in the State just mentioned with a remarkable frequency, which indicated a state of public sentiment altogether peculiar. Besides the benefactors to Harvard University already mentioned, the names of Bartlet, and Norris, and Phillips, and Farrar, will remind you of men who, by their princely munificence, have erected monuments of their liberality which will be long remembered with honour.

I am aware, my dear sons, that you are never likely to be able to do much in the way of endowments in aid of your *Alma Mater*. But if it should please God to prosper you in your worldly circumstances, you may possibly do something to testify your good will and filial regard. And I charge you, if you should ever be able, to give her, either during your lives, or at your decease, some memorial of your gratitude and attachment. If you can do no more, you can probably engage some wealthy acquaintances, who have few or no children, in making a testamentary disposition of their property, to make your college, at least in part, their legatee. And perhaps you yourselves, without doing wrong to any survivor, may leave to her, if it be but a hundred or two dollars, as an humble testimonial of grateful regard. If even this were done by all her alumni who are able to afford it, the amount would, in a few years, invest her with a degree of enlargement and strength greatly conducive to her comfort and usefulness.

No longer ago than last year an alumnus of the College of New Jersey, who was graduated with the class of 1776, and had filled a number of elevated stations in society—left in his last will, as "a testimony of attachment to his venerated *Alma Mater*," one hundred volumes of books, to be selected from his library by a friend whom he named, and added to the library of the college. This was accordingly done; and the legacy was received and acknowledged with marked pleasure by the board of trustees. Why is not something of this kind done more frequently? If every son of the college, who has it in his power, were to do likewise, (and some could, without inconvenience, do much more,) the library of our college would, in a few years, become enlarged to a degree greatly gratifying to all her friends.

The truth is, if all the friends of our college were cordially desirous, and really on the watch, to promote her welfare, they might, with very little effort, accomplish for her an amount of benefit beyond calculation. One, for example, may send to her library, from his own collection, a set of books, or a single volume of rare or curious character. A second, who, in the course of his travels, meets with one or more volumes of great rarity or value, may easily prevail on the owner to present them to the college. A third, at an expense of seven or eight hundred dollars, may establish a fund which shall produce forty or fifty dollars annually to be applied as a premium for ever, and paid to the best classical or mathematical scholar in each class that is graduated. A fourth, who cannot do it himself, may prevail on some acquaintance of larger means, to erect a spacious fire-proof library, which has long been greatly wanted; or a convenient, ornamental chapel, which is equally needed, and which might bear the name of the donor for ever. A fifth, who is fond of some particular science taught in the institution, may be willing to make a large addition to the chemical apparatus, or to present a first-rate telescope, to aid in the study of Astronomy. Why—O why is it that the public spirit, the zeal for the promotion of knowledge which operated so strongly in the minds of our fathers, and produced such honourable results, have so far deserted our country, or at any rate these middle states? I hope, my dear sons, you will do all in your power to revive and extend them, and try to stimulate every high-minded alumnus to become a benefactor, in some way, to his beloved literary mother.

The fact is, every alumnus of a college who travels into foreign countries, might, not only without sacrifice, but with cordial gratification to his honourable feelings, pick up in a hundred places, and bring home with him, specimens of Natural History, models of Engines and Edifices, Casts, Statues, Paintings, Minerals, Coins, Manuscripts, &c., which might be deposited on her shelves, to the great increase of her reputation, and to the enlargement of her means of promoting the improvement of her pupils.

LETTER XX.

PARENTS.

"Indulgentia inepta parentum."—ANON.

MY DEAR SONS—You may feel some surprise that a letter with such a title should be addressed to you. But I should consider this manual as essentially defective, were it not to contain some notice of the bearing of parental influence on the character and conduct of many young men in college. Your own reflections will convince you that this influence is not small, and that it is often far from being happy. It is my wish, therefore, to take this indirect method of reaching the consciences and the hearts of those parents who, perhaps, do more to lead their sons astray than they themselves ever imagined; and whose mischievous influence none but themselves can ever fully correct. For my part, I believe that, in nine cases out of ten, the bad conduct of the young is referable to their parents.

And I begin by remarking, that many parents are so negligent or so unskilful in the original training of their children—if training it may be called—that they can hardly fail to become disorderly members of society, and to prove a perfect nuisance wherever they go. Where children are suffered to grow up without restraint, in the indulgence of every wild freak, and wayward temper; nay, where they are permitted to be the governors of their parents, rather than compelled to submit to their authority, what can be expected of such children, as they advance in age and in stature, but self-will, turbulence, and every species of revolting insubordination? Would it not be something like a miracle, if children thus abandoned to their own corrupt inclinations, should prove otherwise than disorderly and troublesome whenever they attempted to mingle with decent people? The very element of youth thus brought up, may be expected to be insubordination, profaneness, self-indulgence in every form, forgetfulness of truth, and a disregard to the rights and the comfort of others.

Many such young men are sent to college, and there they expect to govern, as they had done at home. There, when not permitted to have their own way in everything, and even to invade the rights of others with impunity, they think themselves hardly and oppressively treated. Nor is a mistake on this subject theirs alone. Their parents are apt to participate in it. And, therefore, when they hear that their sons have drawn upon themselves the discipline of the college, or been sent away from it, they are filled with surprise, and conclude that the faculty must, of course, be to blame. Strange infatuation! Surely the blindness of parental partiality is beyond all bounds! When children are not taught at home to honour and obey their parents; to love and observe domestic order; to regard the truth; to avoid profane language; to pay respect to the feelings of others, what can be expected when they leave home, and are, of course, removed from the eye of their immediate connections? Can there be any rational hope that they will be found comfortable or respectable members of any literary institution to which they may be sent? As well might we expect to "gather grapes of thorns, or figs of thistles." It will be well, indeed, if those who have been taught and trained in the best manner, shall carry with them to the academy and the college, the sentiments and habits which have been inculcated upon them. But where the parental mansion has never resounded with the voice of prayer and praise; where no father's or mother's affection has ever impressed upon their minds, the duty of obedience to the laws under which they are placed; of reverence for God, for the Bible, for the Lord's day, and for everything sacred; and of benevolent regard to the feelings of others, we cannot reasonably hope for anything, from such young people, but insubordination and every evil work. If the result be different, every one who contemplates the circumstance, regards it as a matter of wonder and congratulation.

We are told of an ancient Grecian sage, that, when he saw any young person behaving ill in the street, or in any public place, he immediately went to the house of his parents, and corrected them, as the probable cause of their son's delinquency. The conclusion was wise, and the course taken, rational. When I see a young man noisy, insolent, swaggering, profane, coarse in his manners, and disrespectful to his superiors—I pity him; I spontaneously say within myself—"poor lad! he has had a wretched bringing up; he knows no better;" his parents have either known no better themselves, or they have had neither the principle nor the skill to lead him in the right way; and hence he has grown up "like a wild ass's colt." I verily believe that nine-tenths of all the disobedience to law, and all the consequent disorders in colleges, are to be traced to the unhappy delinquencies of parents; and that no effectual cure of the evil can be expected, but through the medium of parental reformation. Oh, if fathers and mothers—even the most worldly of them—had a just sense of what their sons need in going forth to complete their education; if they made a just estimate of what true politeness is—that it does not consist in fine clothes—in graceful movements, or in a haughty strut and air; but in a deportment at once respectful, benevolent, and adapted to make all around us happy; what a different aspect would all our social circles, and all our literary institutions present! Parents certainly impose a heavy and most unreasonable task on college officers, when they expect them to make scholars and gentlemen of stupid asses, headstrong rebels, and miserable boors, whom they found it impossible either to instruct or govern at home.

But this is not the whole of the evil which flows from parental delinquency. Parents not only send to college young men without any of the qualities which fit them to be either wholesome or comfortable members of a literary institution; without either the decorum or the docility which prepare them to be successful or even tolerable students; but they too often set themselves against the efforts of the faculty, by faithful instruction and discipline, to correct the faults and better the character of their children. It would be distressing to recount the instances in which parents have become grievously offended at measures of the most wise and indispensable kind to promote the welfare of their sons. I have known many cases in which, instead of feeling grateful to the authority of college, for frowning on the gross disorders of their sons, and inflicting the lightest discipline that could be thought of for their offences, they have taken the part of their sons against the authority; considered them as hardly dealt with; and encouraged them to resist the discipline to which they were subjected. The injury done to young men by this conduct on the part of their parents cannot be calculated. How is it possible to conduct discipline with success, when it is thus resisted and reviled by those who ought zealously to sustain it? What encouragement have the officers of such institutions to labour and toil for the benefit of youth, when those who ought to be most grateful to them for their painful efforts, turn against them, and strengthen the hands of their rebellious children?

I must say, my dear sons, that in the course of a long life, I have no recollection of having ever known an instance in which a member of college appeared to me to have been visited with more severe discipline than he deserved. My impression is, that where there is an error in regard to this matter, it is almost always the other way. And, therefore, I give you fair warning beforehand, that if (what I hope will never happen) you should fall under the lash of college authority, you must not expect me to interpose and rescue you from it. I shall take for granted, anterior to all inquiry on the subject, that you richly deserve all you get and more.

An example of noble bearing on this subject once occurred in Princeton, which I cannot forbear to relate, as affording a specimen of what ought much more frequently to be exhibited than we find to be the case. General C——, a highly respectable inhabitant of a neighbouring city, who had himself had two sons educated in our college, and who was, therefore, well acquainted with the institution, happened, some years ago, to be passing through Princeton on the very day in which two students of the college had been suspended and ordered to go home, on account of their disorderly conduct. They came into the hotel, where the General had stopped to refresh himself, and were complaining of the treatment which they had received from the faculty of the college, in a loud manner, and with much foul language. He, at first, was silent; but their vehement complaints being continued, and after a while appearing to be partly addressed to himself—he looked at them with a stern countenance, and said—"Young men, I know nothing of you or your case: but I have long known the Faculty of New Jersey College, and know them to be scholars and gentlemen. I am sure, from your present behaviour, they are in the right, and you in the wrong; and if you were my sons, I would drive you back, with a good cowskin, to the presence of the faculty, and compel you to ask their pardon on your knees." Though the culprits did not know him, yet his age, his commanding figure, and his air of superiority prevented their giving way to resentment. But it is hardly necessary to say, that they slunk out of the apartment abashed and silent.

It is earnestly to be wished, that public sentiment generally, and especially the sentiments and conduct of the leading members of society, might always be found speaking the same language, and taking the part of rightful authority, against juvenile insubordination and insolence. But, alas! this is so far from being the case that, perhaps, no complaint is better founded than that which mourns over the prevalence of an opposite course.

The following remarks by the venerable Bishop Meade, extracted from a publication from his pen noticed in a former letter, are worthy of being solemnly regarded by every parent. "On this subject, let me say one word to parents, in behalf of the schools and colleges in our land. Heavy, indeed, are the complaints of teachers and professors against you in this respect. I hear them wherever I go. You are considered as the great obstacles to the right government of youth in our literary institutions of every grade. Those who have charge of your children declare, that you withhold your support from them in the most trying emergency; that your blind partiality to your sons leads you to receive any statement they may make, or your false views of discipline lead you to palliate, if you do not justify, conduct which is perfectly inadmissible in any well ordered institution. They declare, that it seldom happens that a youth is dismissed, without finding in the parent one to justify him, and condemn them."

There is yet another way in which parents are found not only to injure their sons in college, but also to inflict a serious injury on the character and all the best interests of the institution with which they are connected. I mean by supplying them profusely with money, from time to time, and thus enabling them to gratify their appetites, and tempting them to indulge in freaks of wild disorder, and of mischievous expenditure. This infatuation on the part of the parents, has proved a source of wider and more irreparable mischief than I could easily detail. I am very sure that if parents who have either any reflection or any principle, could be made to understand how deeply such profusion on their part is adapted to injure their sons, and to injure the college, they would no more think of indulging it, than they would the thought of sending to their beloved children, every month, the most virulent poison to be mingled with their daily food.

It is deeply to be deplored that there are, around our colleges, so many persons ready to be mean and criminal purveyors to the appetites of the students; who, in defiance of all the laws of the state, and of the authority of the institutions themselves; nay, in defiance of all the dictates of their own ultimate interest, spread snares for their feet, and lead them on, in many cases, to the breaking up of all their sober habits, and ultimately to their eternal destruction. But the most astonishing and humbling fact of all is, that parents—who have the deepest interest in the welfare of their children, and who might be expected to feel for the well-being of the children of others—cannot be persuaded to frown on those unprincipled conspirators against youth, and to try and make them feel, in the only way in which they seem capable of feeling—I mean in their pockets—that they are engaged in a nefarious traffic which cannot ultimately profit them.

LETTER XXI.

VACATIONS.

Ne mihi otium quidem fuit unquam otiosum.—CICERO.
Simul et jucunda et idonea vitæ.—ANON.

MY DEAR SONS—I know of few things more adapted to draw a distinct and visible line between a wise student and a foolish one, than the occurrence of a vacation. To the latter, who is too commonly a mere *terræ filius*—who has no love to knowledge—who only consented to become a member of a literary institution from mere boyish vanity, or to comply with the wishes of his parents; who desires to enjoy the name of a student, without his toil or his attainments; to him the occurrence of a vacation is the most welcome of all events. He is delighted to escape from study. He is no less gratified, perhaps, to escape from the control and decorum which the supervision of the faculty imposes upon him, and rejoices in the prospect of being able to give himself up, for five or six weeks, to every kind of dissipation that his heart may desire.

Very different from these are the feelings with which a wise and exemplary student contemplates the approach of a recess from study. He rejoices in it, indeed, but not as a period of escape from painful restraint, for he feels none:—not as a season of relief from study; for he loves knowledge, and considers it as a privilege to receive it from the hands of his regular instructors. He looks forward to such an event, however, with real pleasure, as affording him an opportunity to see his friends, and to gratify filial and fraternal affection; to promote his health by an abundance of wholesome exercise; and also to enjoy the privilege of attending to some branches of literary culture which his prescribed tasks may have prevented him from enjoying. For these reasons he looks forward to it with calm and rational pleasure. He takes a temporary leave of the walls of his *Alma Mater* with the decorum and dignity of a gentleman, who respects her, and at the same time respects himself. In travelling to the place of his residence, he is not seen associating with the noisy, the vulgar, and the vile; he is not heard uttering the language of profaneness and brutality, so as to excite the wonder of every decent beholder, where such a young cub could have received his training.

From the foregoing statement you will easily perceive how your father would wish you to meet and to spend your vacations. You will, of course, anticipate them with pleasure. And you will, I hope, contemplate them very much as every wise man regards relaxation from the severer duties of life, as means of refreshment and strength, and of preparation for returning to those duties with renewed alacrity and pleasure. The idea of making a vacation a season of mere vacuity, or of lawless riot, is too ignoble, I trust, to be entertained for a moment by you. You will, I hope, look forward to such a recess as a season of much value, which ought to be carefully improved, and always rendered subservient to some valuable acquisition.

We are told of the celebrated Sir William Jones, that eminent philologist, and master of juridical and oriental learning, that, in his youth, he was in the habit of paying an annual, and sometimes a more frequent visit, of several weeks to London. As that city was his native place, and as he had, of course, from that circumstance, and from the respectability of his character, a large circle of acquaintance there, and was every hour surrounded with scenes of luxury and entertainment, it might have been expected that his visits would have been all devoted to company and amusement. But this amiable and highly cultivated youth was of "another spirit." His impression of the value of knowledge and of time was too deep to allow him thus to employ even a few weeks of recess from prescribed study. He generally, we are told, made each visit to the city subservient to the acquisition of a new language. Why may not you, my dear sons, assign to every vacation which occurs in your college course, the execution of some task which may be of solid use to you as long as you live? For example; when a recess of five or six weeks occurs in the spring, suppose you were to resolve to devote the vacant hours which occur during that time to a careful and thorough perusal of Milton's Paradise Lost, and Paradise Regained; and for that purpose, to take the volumes with you wherever you went, and to study them with that closeness of attention which becomes those who are desirous of being familiar with works of which it is disgraceful to any English scholar to be ignorant. In the vacation of similar extent in the autumn, you may peruse with like attention and profit, the eight volumes of the Spectator, in the pages of which Addison, Steele, and others, who adorned the Augustan age of English literature, made so distinguished a figure. In the vacation of the following spring, let your leisure hours be employed in reading with attention, some of the best parts of Shakspeare's dramas. I say the best parts; for I would not recommend the indiscriminate study of all that goes under the name of that great writer. It is doubtful, as you probably know, whether some of the plays bound up with his works, are really his; and with regard to some others, confidently considered as genuine, they can by no means be recommended as likely to improve either the literary taste or the moral sentiments of those who peruse them. Let your special attention be directed to his Macbeth; his Richard II.; his Henry IV.; Henry V., and Henry VI.; his Richard III.; his Henry VIII.; his King Lear; his Romeo and Juliet; his Hamlet; and his Othello. With these I would advise you to stop; and these, if read as they ought to be, will be more than sufficient to occupy the disposable hours of one vacation. Let the next season of a similar kind be devoted to the perusal of Pope's works; the next to Johnson's Lives of the Poets; and so, in succession, to the other works of Johnson, and to those of Thomson, Goldsmith, Cowper, Beattie, &c., as opportunity may present. If to these you could find time to add Robertson's History of Charles V., Hume's History of England, Hallam's Middle Ages, and the same writer's Constitutional History of England, you would find yourselves greatly profited by the series. How much better to have a system of this sort, than to be at a loss, as many are, during the hours of vacation, how to kill the time; often in perfect ennui, or, perhaps, running over the columns of a newspaper of last year, or of an old almanac, for the sake of guarding against utter vacuity! If this plan, or anything like it, were faithfully persevered in, every student in college, before his regular course was closed, would be familiar with the best masters of sentiment, of diction, and of knowledge that the English language affords.

But perhaps some of your vacations may be spent entirely in travelling. Where this can be done, it may be made not only one of the most interesting, but also one of the most profitable modes of spending a few weeks of recess from regular study. Even then, you may take some classical English volumes with you, and turn the perusal of them to excellent account in the leisure hours which occur in all journeying.

But aside from the opportunities of reading which seldom fail to occur in steamboats, and other vehicles of public conveyance, you ought to remember, that even when you are shut out from these avenues to knowledge, there are others open to you, even by the very circumstances which preclude reading. This is commonly prevented by the crowd of company in which we are placed. But is there nothing to be gained by a vigilant and wise use of this very company as a source of information?

I know, indeed, that reckless young men, intent only on animal gratification, are apt to pass from place to place, when they are travelling, and from one crowded public vehicle to another, without an effort, or even a thought of adding to their stock of knowledge. Whereas, a young man desirous of learning something from every place which he visits, of gleaning instruction from every company into which he is thrown, will be ever on the watch to make the most of every scene through which he passes. He will try to inform himself, even in his most cursory journeyings, of the history, character, and peculiarities of the canals, railroads and turnpikes over which he is borne. He will mark and record the agricultural, the commercial and the manufacturing conditions of every district which he has an opportunity of seeing. He will note well all the internal improvements, the literary, moral, and religious state of every neighbourhood; the numbers, relative strength, prospects, and wants of the different ecclesiastical denominations, and particularly any institutions or practices which may be worthy of imitation. Such a wise youth, in travelling, will always, of course, keep a diary; and if his observation and his notes be such as they ought to be, he will return from every journey with an amount of new information, richer and more vividly impressed on the mind than he could possibly gain from books.

Not only so; but in every such journey an attentive traveller, who is on the watch for incidents and sources of improvement, will, of course, fall in with companions in travel, from whom he may learn much which books would never teach him. He will, probably, seldom enter a crowded public vehicle without meeting with one and another who have visited remote parts of the world, and from whom he might derive information, imparted with all the impressiveness which the living speaker, and the animated countenance can alone confer. In such circumstances, in almost every journey, a young traveller, if awake to the opportunities of instruction, may collect an amount of information concerning foreign countries—concerning Rome or Athens, concerning Palestine and Jerusalem, concerning Egypt, and Cairo, and the Pyramids, &c.—for which he would look in vain in any printed volume. Why is it that so few young men, who have life before them; who might be benefited as well as adorned by such information; and who might gather up by handfuls instructive facts concerning every part of the world, are so little awake to the value of the privilege, and so little disposed to avail themselves of the advantages which it offers? It is evident that in this way the travels of others may be made substantially their own.

Thus you see, my dear sons, that wherever you may spend your vacations—whether at home, or in journeying; whether among friends or strangers, it will be your own fault if you do not make them truly and richly profitable. Surely to have an opportunity of reading valuable works which could not be read during term-time; or to visit different parts of the country; or to see more of the world; or to converse with different classes of men—are advantages which will be lightly esteemed by none, who have minds capable of making the estimate.

When, therefore, I see a student reckless of all these advantages, the moment a vacation begins, trying to escape from all reading, as having had too much of it in term-time; flying from the company of the grave and the wise, from whom he might learn much, and frequenting the haunts of the dissipated and disorderly; everywhere smoking, drinking and racketing with the children of folly; when I see this, I instinctively regard such a young man as "void of understanding;" lost to himself and his friends; and as much more likely to prove a disgrace than an honour to the place of his education.

LETTER XXII.

MISCELLANEOUS THOUGHTS—CONCLUSION.

Let us hear the conclusion of the whole matter; fear God, and keep his commandments; for this is the whole duty of man.—Eccles. xii. 13.

My Dear Sons—I have now touched as briefly, and yet as pointedly as I know how, on the leading topics which appear to me to be peculiarly interesting to you as students in college. I would fain hope that I have gained your assent to every successive remark as I went along. But of one thing I am confident, that you will give me credit for having uttered my sincere and unbiassed convictions in all that I have said. You cannot suspect me of a sinister design in any one of the counsels which occupy the foregoing pages. No, my sons, I have no desire to damp the sanguine joy, or cloud the smiling sun of your youth. I would not take from you a single rational pleasure. On the contrary, I delight to see you happy; and desire, by all the means in my power, to promote your true enjoyment and honour. But you must allow me now, in my advanced life, when I have seen so much of the illusions of the world, and so many examples of the destruction of those who yielded to them, to counsel you, not in the style of youthful flattery, but in the language of "truth and soberness." I have not attempted to carry a point with you by overpainting, or by any other artifice. If you have a real disinterested friend on earth, who unfeignedly wishes to promote your interests in both worlds, it is he who has penned the foregoing letters. And in publishing them for the benefit of others, I have endeavoured to put myself, in thought, in the place of the parents and guardians of all your fellow students, and to speak to them all as my own beloved children. I have not given a counsel or an injunction but what I conscientiously believe, if followed, will be for your benefit, as a candidate for success and happiness in this world, as well as an immortal being. Nay, I have not given a counsel but what I am verily persuaded your own judgment will sanction, twenty years hence, if you should live so long, and which, if you neglect it, will be matter of bitter self-reproach to you to the end of life.

I have been young, my dear sons, and now am old. I have been, as you know, a member of a college, as you now are; and, of course, I know something of the habits, the follies, the prejudices, the snares and dangers with which you are surrounded. Now, when I have laid open my whole heart to you concerning these matters, and have told you, with all the conscientiousness of truth, and with all the tenderness of parental affection, how these things appear to me in the decline of life, and in view of my final account, will you not listen to me?

Perhaps, in the fulness of your filial feelings, you may be ready, after reading what has been written, to say—"All these counsels are right; all these things will we do." But, rely upon it, to carry this resolution into effect will not be so easy as you imagine. The rashness of inexperience; the impetuosity of youthful feeling; the sudden burst of passion; the folly and violence of companions in study—all—all endanger, every day, the overthrow of your discretion; and may, in an unexpected hour, as it were, spring a mine under your feet, and disconcert, before you are aware, all those plans of order which in your calmer moments you had adopted, and determined to follow. Under these impressions, allow me to close this letter, and this whole manual, with a few counsels, which a heart most anxious for your welfare, as long as it shall continue to beat, will not cease to pray, may be deeply impressed upon your minds: and

1. Be not confident of your own power to do all that your judgment tells you is right; all that you have resolved to do, in conformity with the foregoing letters. Your feelings are sometimes strong, and in an evil hour, may overpower your judgment. Your inclinations, never to be implicitly trusted, may run counter to your duty and get the victory; and some plausible fellow student, less worthy of respect than you have hitherto thought him, may set a trap and ensnare you, before you are aware, and may involve you in a difficulty from which retreat is not easy. On all these accounts, and others too numerous to be specified in detail, be not confident that it will be an easy thing to adhere to your resolutions, and to perform all the duties which your judgment tells you ought to be performed, by wise and orderly students.

2. If you feel your own weakness, and the power of temptation in any measure as you ought, you will be disposed to look for aid from above, and to pray without ceasing for the guidance and strength which you need. Whenever any exigency arises which requires decision, especially if it involves any question of difficulty, be not in haste to act. Pause, reflect, and calculate both probable and possible consequences. Ask direction from your father's and mother's God. And if the path of duty be still doubtful, take that course which will be obviously safe, rather than that which is adapted to gratify a spirit of vanity and youthful display. It is the counsel of prudence, as well as of holy scripture, "acknowledge God in all your ways, and he will direct your steps."

I should feel, my dear sons, as if I had gained much, if I could find you deeply impressed with a sense of your danger of being led astray, and of your constant need of guidance and aid from above. Nothing less, you may rest assured, will suffice for your protection. We may speculate, and philosophize, and prescribe as much as we please about other remedies for the corrupt tendencies and temptations of the young; but they will all be vain. "The strong man armed" can never be overcome and cast out, but by one stronger than he. We may tell young men, every day that we live, of the wisdom and happiness of virtue. We may demonstrate to them with all the force of reasoning, and with all the power of eloquence, that the path of temperance, of diligence in study, and of undeviating regularity in every respect, is the wisest course. We may assure them that it is as much their happiness and their honour as it is their duty, to be all that their instructors can require or wish. We may tell them all this; and they may fully believe us. Nay, they know that it is so. Their judgments and their consciences are decisively in favour of it all. But, alas! their hearts are not gained. In spite of all that we can say, when passion pleads; when the syren voice of pleasure calls, away they will hasten "as an ox goeth to the slaughter." The admonitions of conscience are either not heard at all, or, if heard, speedily silenced by the overflowing tide of youthful feeling. Alas! how many young men, whose sober convictions, when consulted, are strongly on the side of what is right, have, notwithstanding, from the mere influence of appetite and passion, or the impulse of still more inflamed and infatuated companions, in an evil hour, plunged irretrievably into courses which have destroyed them, soul and body, for ever! O how constantly and importunately ought those who are exposed to such temptations and perils, to implore that guardianship which can alone guide them aright!

3. Recollect that you are every day forming habits and establishing a character, which will probably follow you through life. The great difficulty of most students is, that they "do not consider." They cannot be persuaded to lay to heart the importance of

every day they live, and of every opportunity they enjoy. They have but one life to live. The precious time which is now passing, and the privileges with which they are now favoured, can never return. O, if young men could be induced to "consider their ways;" to "look before they leap;" to reflect seriously before they act; and to prize as they ought the price now put into their hands for getting wisdom; how many of their false steps would be prevented! How many of those deplorable calamities which cloud their course, and pain the hearts of parents, would be happily averted!

4. Think how easy it is, in the outset, to avoid being implicated in the disorders of a college, compared with what it is in the progress of the mischief. In the commencement of such disorder, one simple rule, like a perfect panacea, will deliver you from all embarrassment. That rule is, without any reference to its character or its aim, to have no connection with it; to decline attending its meetings; signing its papers, or concurring in its applications. By abstaining, kindly and respectfully, but firmly, from all participation in the proposed movement, no harm can be done in any case: whereas in allowing yourselves to be implicated in a movement which in the outset may appear perfectly innocent, you may be unexpectedly drawn into a vortex of disgrace and ruin. What was only intended to be a piece of harmless merriment, or a respectful request, has, perhaps, insensibly grown into a combination of infatuated rebels. "Behold how great a matter a little fire kindleth!"

Shall we never have done with scenes of insubordination and disorder in our colleges? Are students in our highest literary institutions more unreasonable and perverse than other young men? Are they less accessible to ingenuous sentiments; less open to conviction from the plainest reasoning; less desirous of happiness; less capable of elevated and manly feelings than others of their age differently situated? It cannot be. Surely the air of a college cannot, as a matter of course, inebriate all who breathe it. Surely the walls of a college cannot blind and stultify all who inhabit them. Surely college students, the moment they become such, cannot be at once transformed into such miserable cowards, or such incorrigible fools, as, of course, like a flock of silly sheep, to follow in the train of every ruffian blockhead who chooses to leap over a precipice, and destroy himself. Why, then, does it so often happen, that those young men who, under the parental roof, were amiable, ingenuous, and docile; after being advanced to the higher privileges, and more enlarged instruction of a college, are so apt to become blinded by passion, the sport of childish feeling, and more disposed than before to "call evil good, and good evil; to put darkness for light, and light for darkness; to put bitter for sweet, and sweet for bitter?" *Causa latet, vis est notissima.* And yet, I know not that the cause is really hidden. The gregarious principle, which, when sanctified, is productive of so much good, may become, when perverted, a source of incalculable evil. Hence it so often happens that associated bodies, in the fervour of their feelings, and in the madness of their spasmodic excitements, are found to do things of which any individual of their whole number would be utterly ashamed.

Can you, for a moment, doubt, my beloved sons, that it is as much your interest as it is your duty, to be perfectly exemplary in all your relations to the college of which you are members? Can you doubt that it will be for your own happiness and honour to obey every law of the institution; to perform all your prescribed tasks with diligence and faithfulness; and to treat every one both within and without its walls with the urbanity of perfect gentlemen? I am sure you cannot and do not doubt concerning one jot or tittle of all this. Why, then, O why are these principles really and faithfully acted upon by only one in ten or twenty of the students of any college in our land? I could sit down and weep when I learn, from day to day, from so many channels of public intelligence, and from colleges in almost every quarter of our country, of masses of students who appear as if their constant and supreme study was how they might most effectually secure their own disgrace and misery, and render those around them also as miserable as possible.

Cannot young gentlemen, in circumstances so conspicuous and responsible, be persuaded to appreciate their own interest? Can they not be prevailed upon, if they will not respect others, at least to respect themselves; to respect public opinion, to which they look for high honours, and on which they rely for that brilliant success which, as a matter of course, they anticipate for themselves. Above all, can they not be persuaded to respect that high and holy One, whose favour is life, and whose loving kindness is better than life? If they consider it as an honourable achievement to deceive and overreach the faculty, can they regard in a similar light that conduct which degrades themselves, and is a prelude to inevitable shame? Alas! for the infatuation of young men who can glory in their own dishonour, and boast of intellectual and moral suicide!

When I compare what young men might gain in college, with what they usually do gain, the contrast is most humiliating. Instead of striving to enrich their minds with every kind of literary and scientific acquirement adapted to prepare them for an elevated and honourable course in life; instead of labouring to gather knowledge by handfuls, and to make every session a source of intellectual wealth; how many act as if their object were to gain a diploma to which they had no title; to cheat themselves and their parents by clutching a mere barren parchment!

Here, my dear sons, I must take my leave of you, and close these counsels. And yet I scarcely know how to lay aside my pen. Not that I feel as if I had anything new, or more weighty than has been already expressed, to say; but because I scarcely know how to tear myself away from the chair of affectionate, paternal counsel, or cease to exhort and entreat, when I feel that so much may depend on "a word in season" to those whose habits and character are forming. But to the God of your parents, I must now commit you. May he be your protector and your guide! This shall be the unceasing prayer of your affectionate friend and father,

SAMUEL MILLER.

PRINCETON, *February* 1*st*, 1843.

THE END.

www.ingramcontent.com/pod-product-compliance
Lightning Source LLC
LaVergne TN
LVHW050518100826
845148LV00002B/379

* 9 7 8 1 4 2 5 5 2 0 5 4 0 *